Mastering the Stock Market: The Proven Strategy to Build Wealth and Minimize Risk

A Step-by-Step Guide to Picking Profitable Stocks and Achieving Financial Freedom

NATAN STERLING

(S)

Staten House

ISBN:979-8-89965-140-3

TABLE OF CONTENTS

INTRODUCTION

Why Investing in Stocks is the Key to Financial Freedom

The stock market has long been one of the most powerful tools for building wealth, yet many people remain hesitant to invest. Some believe it is too risky, others think it is too complicated, and many assume that successful investing requires years of experience or a degree in finance. The reality, however, is that anyone can learn how to invest wisely—if they have the right approach.

The biggest misconception about investing is that it is all about luck, timing, or insider knowledge. You have heard stories of people who made millions overnight by picking the right stock at the right moment. While those stories exist, they are rare exceptions, not the rule. The truth is long-term success in investing is not about gambling—it is about following a proven system that allows you to make informed decisions with confidence. Many people delay investing because they believe they need a large amount of money to get started. But waiting is one of the biggest mistakes you can make. The earlier you start, the more you benefit from compound growth, which is the most powerful force in wealth creation. Even small, consistent investments can lead to substantial financial gains over time. For example, investing just $100 per month with an average annual return of 10% (which is historically the stock market's long-term average) could turn into $100,000 in 30 years. If you wait another ten years to start, that amount is cut in half. Time is your greatest asset, and this book will show you how to make the most of it.

Why This Book is Different

There are thousands of investing books available, but most of them fall into one of two categories. Some are overly technical, filled with complex financial jargon and theories that make them inaccessible to beginners. Others are too vague, offering general advice like "buy good companies" without explaining how to identify them.

This book takes a different approach. It is designed to be practical, clear, and actionable. You do not need a financial background to understand it. Instead of overwhelming you with unnecessary details, I will give you a simple, repeatable 4-step formula that will allow you to find great stocks in just 15 minutes.

This system is based on real-world investing principles used by some of the greatest investors in history, including Warren Buffett, Peter Lynch, and Nassim Taleb. You will learn how to analyse stocks quickly, determine the right time to buy and sell, avoid costly mistakes, and build a portfolio that grows over time.

What You Will Learn

The goal of this book is to transform you from a hesitant beginner into a confident investor. You will learn how to:

- Understand the basics of the stock market so you can invest with confidence.
- Identify winning stocks using a simple 4-step formula that takes just 15 minutes per stock.
- Know exactly when to buy and sell to maximize your profits.
- Avoid common investing mistakes that cause most people to lose money.
- Develop a long-term strategy that allows you to grow wealth with minimal stress.

By the time you finish this book, you will have a clear roadmap for making smart investment decisions without spending hours analysing financial statements or following every twist and turn of the market.

Who This Book is For

This book is for anyone who wants to invest in stocks but does not know where to start. Whether you are a complete beginner or someone who has dabbled in investing but never felt fully confident in your strategy, this book will give you the tools and knowledge to invest wisely.

If you are looking for a get-rich-quick scheme, this book is not for you. Successful investing requires patience, discipline, and a focus on long-term growth, not short-term speculation. However, if you are willing to follow a proven strategy and invest consistently, you will see real, lasting results.

The Power of Starting Now

How to Get the Most Out of This Book

To ensure you absorb and apply the knowledge in this book, I encourage you to take an active approach. As you read, try analysing stocks in real time, using the 4-step formula that I will outline in the coming chapters. If you are completely new to investing, do not worry—I will guide you through the process step by step.

By the end of this book, you will have everything you need to confidently choose great stocks, know when to buy and sell, and build a portfolio that grows over time. You do not need to be an expert to succeed in investing—you just need the right strategy and the discipline to follow it.

Now, let us get started. Your journey to financial freedom begins now.

CHAPTER 1 – STOCK MARKET BASICS FOR BEGINNERS

Investing in the stock market can seem intimidating at first, especially with all the financial jargon, complex charts, and conflicting advice. Many beginners hesitate to get started because they fear losing money or making the wrong choices. However, the reality is that the stock market is one of the most powerful wealth-building tools available, and understanding the basics is the first step toward making smart investment decisions.

At its core, the stock market is simply a marketplace where investors buy and sell ownership stakes in companies. When you purchase a share of a company's stock, you are buying a small piece of that company. As the company grows and becomes more profitable, the value of your shares increases, allowing you to build wealth over time. Conversely, if the company performs poorly or market conditions change, the value of your shares may decline. This fluctuation in stock prices is what makes the stock market both an opportunity and a challenge.

There are two main ways to make money in the stock market: capital appreciation and dividends. Capital appreciation occurs when the price of a stock increases over time, allowing investors to sell their shares for a profit. For example, if you buy a stock at $50 per share and sell it later for $100, you have doubled your investment. Dividends, on the other hand, are payments that some companies distribute to their shareholders as a share of their profits. Companies that offer dividends typically do so on a regular basis, providing investors with a steady stream of passive income.

One of the key principles of successful investing is understanding the difference between short-term fluctuations and long-term trends. Stock prices can be highly volatile in the short term, influenced by economic news, political events, and market sentiment. However, over the long term, the stock market has historically trended upward, rewarding patient investors who stay invested and avoid making impulsive decisions based on temporary market movements.

A common mistake many beginners make is trying to time the market, attempting to buy stocks at their lowest points and sell them at their peaks. While this strategy may seem logical, it is impossible to execute consistently. Even professional investors struggle to predict short-term market movements with accuracy. Instead of trying to time the market, a more effective approach is to invest regularly and focus on high-quality companies with strong fundamentals.

There are diverse types of stocks that serve various investment goals.

Growth stocks are companies that reinvest most of their earnings to expand rapidly, often prioritizing innovation and market expansion over short-term profitability. These stocks tend to have higher volatility but can offer significant returns for investors willing to take on more risk. Value stocks, on the other hand, are companies that are considered undervalued compared to their intrinsic worth. These stocks often pay dividends and attract investors looking for stability and consistent returns. Dividend stocks provide regular income through dividend payments, making them a popular choice for those seeking passive income.

Another important concept in stock investing is diversification. Placing all your money into a single stock can be highly risky because the fate of your investment depends entirely on the performance of that one company. A diversified portfolio, which includes a mix of stocks from different industries and sectors, reduces risk and increases the likelihood of stable long-term growth. Exchange-Traded Funds (ETFs) and index funds are excellent tools for achieving diversification, allowing investors to own a broad selection of stocks with a single investment.

Understanding the role of the broader economy in stock market performance is also crucial. Interest rates, inflation, economic growth, and corporate earnings all impact stock prices. When interest rates rise, borrowing becomes more expensive, which can slow down corporate growth and lead to lower stock prices. Inflation reduces the purchasing power of money, affecting consumer spending and company profits. Economic growth, measured by indicators like GDP, influences investor confidence and overall market performance. Recognizing these factors helps investors make informed decisions and anticipate market trends.

The stock market operates through major exchanges such as the New York Stock Exchange (NYSE) and the Nasdaq, where companies list their shares for public trading. These exchanges provide liquidity, allowing investors to buy and sell stocks efficiently. Stocks are bought and sold through brokerage accounts, which function as intermediaries between investors and the stock market. Today, online brokerage platforms have made investing more accessible than ever, with commission-free trading and user-friendly interfaces that simplify the process.

One of the most fundamental principles of investing is distinguishing between speculation and true investing. Speculation involves high-risk bets on short-term price movements, often driven by hype or market trends. Investing, on the other hand, is a long-term strategy based on thorough research and a disciplined approach. Successful investors focus on companies with strong financials, sustainable competitive advantages, and growth potential, rather than chasing quick profits or following market fads.

Education is the foundation of successful investing. The more you learn about how the stock market works, the better equipped you will be to make smart financial decisions. Many legendary investors, including Warren Buffett, emphasize the importance of continuous learning and patience. Investing is not about making quick gains but about building sustainable wealth over time.

As you move forward in this book, you will learn a structured, repeatable method for selecting the best stocks, analysing their financial health, and determining the right time to buy and sell. The key to success in the stock market is not luck or perfect timing but following a proven system with discipline and confidence. By mastering the fundamentals outlined in this chapter, you are laying the groundwork for long-term financial success and setting yourself up to become a knowledgeable, strategic investor.

.1 How Stocks and the Stock Market Work: A Simple Guide

The stock market is one of the most powerful tools for building wealth, yet many people are intimidated by its complexity. The stock market operates on a simple principle: it is a marketplace where people buy and sell ownership stakes in companies. Understanding how it works is the first step toward making smart investment decisions and growing your wealth over time.

At its core, the stock market exists to help businesses raise money and allow investors to own a share of a company's success. Companies issue stocks to raise capital, which they can use for expansion, research, or other business activities. When you buy a stock, you are purchasing a small piece of that company—also known as a share. If the company grows and becomes more profitable, the value of your shares increases, allowing you to sell them for a higher price than what you initially paid. On the other hand, if the company struggles or the market declines, your shares may lose value.

The stock market operates through major exchanges, such as the New York Stock Exchange (NYSE) and the Nasdaq, where companies list their shares for public trading. These exchanges function as an auction house, matching buyers with sellers to facilitate smooth transactions. Stock prices fluctuate throughout the day based on supply and demand. When more investors want to buy a stock than sell it, the price goes up. When more investors are selling than buying, the price goes down.

Stocks are classified into distinct categories based on their characteristics. Common stocks give shareholders voting rights in the company and potential dividends, while preferred stocks offer higher dividend payouts but usually without voting rights. Investors also distinguish between growth stocks, value stocks, and dividend stocks.

Growth stocks belong to companies that are expanding rapidly, often reinvesting profits rather than paying dividends. Value stocks are considered undervalued compared to their intrinsic worth and may offer stable returns over time. Dividend stocks distribute a portion of the company's earnings to shareholders, providing consistent passive income.

The overall performance of the stock market is measured by stock indexes such as the S&P 500, Dow Jones Industrial Average, and Nasdaq Composite. These indexes track a collection of stocks and provide a snapshot of how the market is performing. When people say, "the market is up" or "the market is down," they are often referring to these indexes.

One of the most important aspects of stock investing is liquidity, which refers to how easily a stock can be bought or sold without significantly affecting its price. Highly traded stocks, such as those from major companies like Apple and Microsoft, are highly liquid, meaning you can buy or sell shares quickly. Smaller or less well-known companies may have lower liquidity, making it harder to execute trades at your desired price.

Investors participate in the stock market through brokerage accounts, which function as intermediaries between buyers and sellers. Online brokers such as Robinhood, Fidelity, Charles Schwab, and TD Ameritrade have made investing more accessible than ever, allowing individuals to buy and sell stocks with just a few clicks. Many of these platforms offer commission-free trading, real-time data, and research tools to help investors make informed decisions.

Another key element of the stock market is market capitalization, which refers to the total value of a company's outstanding shares. Companies are classified into distinct categories based on their market cap. Large-cap stocks (companies worth over $10 billion) are typically well-established businesses with stable earnings. Mid-cap stocks ($2 billion to $10 billion) represent companies in a phase of significant growth. Small-cap stocks (under \$2 billion) are often younger companies with high growth potential but also higher risk.

Stock prices fluctuate for several reasons, including company earnings, economic conditions, and investor sentiment. Earnings reports, released quarterly, provide insight into a company's profitability and growth potential. A strong earnings report can boost a stock's price, while disappointing results can cause a decline. Economic factors such as inflation, interest rates, and global events also influence stock prices. For example, when interest rates rise, borrowing costs increase, which can slow down economic growth and impact stock performance.

Investors use different strategies to participate in the stock market. Some prefer long-term investing, buying stocks in strong companies and holding them for years or even decades. Others engage in trading, where they buy and sell stocks frequently, aiming to profit from short-term price fluctuations. Long-term investing, often referred to as buy and hold, is widely considered the safest and most effective strategy for building wealth over time.

One common misconception is that you need a lot of money to start investing in stocks. The reality is that anyone can start investing with as little as \$10 or \$100. Many brokerage platforms now offer fractional shares, allowing investors to buy a portion of a stock rather than a full share. This makes it easier to invest in high-priced stocks like Amazon or Tesla, even with a small budget.

Understanding how the stock market works is essential for making informed investment decisions. The market is not a casino; it is a tool for long-term wealth building. By learning the fundamentals and adopting a strategic approach, you can take advantage of the stock market's potential and grow your financial future with confidence.

.2ETFs vs. Individual Stocks: Which is Better for You?

When it comes to investing in the stock market, one of the biggest decisions you will face is whether to invest in individual stocks or exchange-traded funds (ETFs). Both options have their advantages and disadvantages, and choosing the right one depends on your investment goals, risk tolerance, and experience level. To make an informed decision, it is important to understand how each works and how they can fit into your portfolio.

What Are Individual Stocks?

Investing in individual stocks means purchasing shares of a specific company. When you buy stock in a company like Apple, Tesla, or Amazon, you own a small part of that business. Your returns depend on the company's performance—if the company grows and becomes more profitable, the value of your shares increases, and if the company underperforms, your shares lose value.

Advantages of Investing in Individual Stocks

One of the biggest advantages of investing in individual stocks is the potential for higher returns. If you pick the right stocks, you can significantly outperform the overall market. For example, early investors in Amazon or Apple saw their investments grow exponentially over the years.

Another key advantage is control. When you invest in individual stocks, you get to decide exactly which companies you want to own, how much to invest in each, and when to buy or sell. This level of control allows investors to tailor their portfolios to their specific preferences, whether they want to focus on high-growth technology companies, dividend-paying stocks, or undervalued companies with strong fundamentals.

Another benefit is dividends. Some companies pay dividends—regular cash payments to shareholders—providing a steady stream of passive income. This can be especially appealing to long-term investors looking for consistent returns.

Disadvantages of Investing in Individual Stocks

Despite the potential for high returns, investing in individual stocks comes with higher risk. A single company's performance can be affected by numerous factors, including poor management, declining industry trends, competition, or unexpected economic downturns. If you invest heavily in one company and it underperforms, your entire portfolio could suffer significant losses.

Additionally, picking individual stocks requires extensive research and ongoing monitoring. Unlike ETFs, which are designed to spread risk across multiple stocks, investing in a single company requires understanding its financial health, leadership, market position, and long-term growth potential. This can be time-consuming and overwhelming, especially for beginners.

Another major downside is lack of diversification. If you only invest in a few individual stocks, your portfolio is highly dependent on those companies' performance. Even if one stock does exceptionally well, others may not, which can lead to significant fluctuations in your portfolio's value.

What Are ETFs?

An Exchange-Traded Fund (ETF) is a basket of stocks, bonds, or other assets that trades on the stock market like a single stock. When you invest in an ETF, you are buying shares in a diversified portfolio of investments. ETFs are designed to track a specific index, sector, or investment strategy, providing investors with instant diversification.

For example, the S&P 500 ETF (SPY) tracks the performance of the top 500 companies in the U.S. stock market. By investing in this ETF, you gain exposure to a wide range of industries and companies without needing to pick individual stocks.

Advantages of Investing in ETFs

One of the biggest advantages of ETFs is diversification. Because ETFs hold multiple stocks, they spread risk across different companies, industries, and sometimes even countries. This reduces the impact of deficient performance from any single company, making ETFs a safer option for beginners and conservative investors.

Another key benefit is simplicity. Instead of researching and selecting individual stocks, you can invest in an ETF that automatically includes a diversified mix of investments. This makes ETFs an excellent choice for people who do not have the time or expertise to analyse individual companies.

ETFs are also known for lower costs and fees. Many ETFs have lower expense ratios compared to actively managed mutual funds, and most brokerage platforms now offer commission-free ETF trades. This makes ETFs a cost-effective way to invest.

Additionally, ETFs are highly liquid, meaning they can be bought and sold throughout the trading day at market prices. This flexibility allows investors to react quickly to market changes and adjust their portfolios as needed.

Disadvantages of Investing in ETFs

While ETFs offer many benefits, they also have some drawbacks. One potential downside is limited control. When you invest in an ETF, you do not get to pick the specific stocks within the fund. Instead, you are investing in a pre-selected group of stocks chosen by the fund's managers or based on an index. This means you may end up holding stocks you would not have chosen individually.

Another disadvantage is that ETFs are designed to track the market, not beat it. While ETFs provide steady long-term growth, they typically will not deliver the kind of explosive gains that individual stocks can. If you are looking for high returns, investing in individual stocks may be a better option.

Some ETFs also come with management fees, which, although typically low, can still reduce overall returns. While index-based ETFs tend to have exceptionally low fees, actively managed ETFs can be more expensive.

Which is Better for You: ETFs or Individual Stocks?

Deciding between ETFs and individual stocks depends on your investment goals, risk tolerance, and experience level. If you are new to investing, want a low-maintenance, diversified portfolio, and prefer steady long-term growth, ETFs are an excellent choice. They allow you to invest in a broad range of stocks with minimal effort and lower risk.

On the other hand, if you enjoy researching companies, want to take a more hands-on approach, and are willing to accept higher risk in exchange for the possibility of higher returns, investing in individual stocks may be a better fit.

Some investors choose to combine both strategies by holding a core portfolio of ETFs for stability while also investing in individual stocks to seek higher returns. This hybrid approach allows for diversification while still taking advantage of potential high-growth opportunities.

Both ETFs and individual stocks have their place in an investment portfolio. ETFs offer diversification, simplicity, and lower risk, making them ideal for long-term investors who prefer a hands-off approach. Individual stocks provide the opportunity for higher returns and greater control but require extensive research and come with more risk.

The best approach is to align your investment strategy with your financial goals. If you are just starting out, consider using ETFs as your foundation while gradually adding individual stocks as you gain experience. Regardless of your choice, the most important thing is to start investing and stay committed to a long-term plan.

Understanding the strengths and weaknesses of both ETFs and individual stocks will help you build a portfolio that suits your risk tolerance and financial aspirations. With the right approach, you can take full advantage of the stock market's potential and work toward achieving your long-term financial goals.

.3Technical vs. Fundamental Analysis: Which Strategy Works Best?

Investors use two main strategies to evaluate stocks: technical analysis and fundamental analysis. Each method offers a unique approach to analysing the stock market, and choosing the right one depends on an investor's goals, experience, and investment style. Understanding these two strategies can help investors make more informed decisions and build a portfolio that aligns with their financial objectives.

What is Fundamental Analysis?

Fundamental analysis focuses on evaluating a company's financial health, business model, and long-term growth potential. This method involves studying financial statements, earnings reports, industry trends, and economic conditions to determine whether a stock is undervalued, priced, or overvalued. The goal is to identify companies with strong fundamentals that can generate consistent profits over time.

Investors who use fundamental analysis look at key financial metrics such as revenue, earnings per share (EPS), price-to-earnings ratio (P/E), and return on equity (ROE) to assess a company's financial stability. They also analyse a company's competitive advantage, management team, and market position to predict its long-term success.

For example, a company with strong earnings growth, low debt, and a solid business model is often considered a worthwhile investment, regardless of short-term stock price fluctuations. Fundamental analysts believe that a company's stock price will eventually reflect its true value, so they focus on long-term investing rather than short-term price movements.

Advantages of Fundamental Analysis

One of the biggest advantages of fundamental analysis is that it helps investors make informed, long-term decisions. Instead of reacting to short-term market fluctuations, fundamental investors base their decisions on a company's actual financial performance and growth potential. This approach reduces the impact of market speculation and allows investors to build a portfolio of high-quality stocks with strong long-term potential.

Another advantage is that fundamental analysis can help investors identify undervalued stocks—companies that are trading below their intrinsic value. Buying undervalued stocks allows investors to benefit when the market eventually recognizes the company's true worth, leading to potential price appreciation.

Fundamental analysis is also widely used by professional investors and institutions, including legendary investors like Warren Buffett, who rely on company fundamentals to make investment decisions.

Challenges of Fundamental Analysis

One of the main challenges of fundamental analysis is that it requires time and effort. Analysing financial statements, industry reports, and macroeconomic trends can be complex and overwhelming for beginners. It also requires patience, as the market may take time to reflect a company's true value.

Additionally, fundamental analysis does not always account for short-term market movements. Even a strong company can experience stock price declines due to economic downturns, investor sentiment, or unexpected events. Investors who rely solely on fundamentals must be prepared for market volatility and focus on the long-term perspective.

What is Technical Analysis?

Technical analysis takes a different approach by focusing on price charts, trends, and trading volume rather than a company's financials. This method assumes that all available information is already reflected in a stock's price and that historical price movements can be used to predict future trends.

Technical analysts use chart patterns, indicators, and statistical tools to identify entry and exit points for trades. Common tools in technical analysis include:

- **Moving Averages (MA):** Helps smooth out price trends and identify potential reversals.
- **Relative Strength Index (RSI):** Measures whether a stock is overbought or oversold.
- **Support and Resistance Levels:** Identifies price levels where a stock is likely to bounce or reverse.
- **Candlestick Patterns**: Provides insights into short-term price movements based on past price action.

Technical traders do not focus on a company's financial statements or business fundamentals. Instead, they rely on patterns, trends, and momentum indicators to make short-term trading decisions. This makes technical analysis particularly popular among day traders and swing traders who aim to profit from short-term price fluctuations.

Advantages of Technical Analysis

One of the key advantages of technical analysis is that it provides immediate trading signals. Unlike fundamental analysis, which requires deep research into a company's financials, technical analysis allows traders to make quick decisions based on price patterns and trends.

Another advantage is that technical analysis can be used for short-term trading strategies, making it a preferred method for active traders. By identifying support and resistance levels, traders can time their trades to maximize profits and minimize losses.

Technical analysis also applies to multiple asset classes, including stocks, cryptocurrencies, forex, and commodities. Since it focuses on price movements rather than company fundamentals, it can be used across different markets and industries.

Challenges of Technical Analysis

A major challenge of technical analysis is that it relies heavily on historical price data, which does not always guarantee future performance. While price patterns and trends can provide useful insights, unexpected market events or external factors can disrupt predictions.

Another limitation is that technical analysis is highly subjective. Different traders may interpret the same chart differently, leading to inconsistent results. This makes it difficult to develop a fully reliable strategy based solely on technical analysis.

Additionally, technical trading often involves frequent buying and selling, which can lead to higher transaction costs and potential tax implications. Active traders must also be disciplined to avoid emotional trading, which can lead to impulsive decisions and increased risk.

Which Strategy is Better?

The choice between fundamental and technical analysis depends on an investor's goals, risk tolerance, and investment horizon.

Fundamental analysis is ideal for long-term investors who want to invest in high-quality companies with strong financials and growth potential. It requires patience and research but can lead to sustainable wealth building over time.

Technical analysis, on the other hand, is better suited for short-term traders who seek to capitalize on price movements. It provides quick decision-making tools but requires discipline and risk management to be effective.

Many investors choose to combine both strategies to improve their decision-making. For example, an investor may use fundamental analysis to identify strong companies and technical analysis to determine the best entry points. This hybrid approach can help balance long-term growth potential with short-term trading opportunities.

Both fundamental and technical analysis offer valuable insights into the stock market, but their effectiveness depends on how they are used. Fundamental analysis helps investors focus on the long-term strength of a company, while technical analysis provides short-term signals for trading opportunities.

The best strategy depends on your personal investing style. If you are looking for long-term wealth accumulation, fundamental analysis may be the better approach. If you prefer active trading and short-term profits, technical analysis could be more suitable.

Understanding the strengths and weaknesses of both methods will help you make better investment decisions. By applying the right strategy for your goals, you can maximize returns while managing risk effectively in the stock market

CHAPTER 2 – HOW TO PICK THE BEST STOCKS IN 15 MINUTES

Investing in individual stocks can be overwhelming, especially when faced with thousands of options and endless financial data. Many investors spend weeks analysing a single company, yet others make decisions in minutes. The reality is that picking great stocks does not have to be complicated or time-consuming. With the right method, you can quickly filter out weak stocks and focus on companies with strong financials, growth potential, and competitive advantages—all in just 15 minutes.

The key to successful stock selection is eliminating unnecessary complexity and focusing on the most crucial factors that drive a company's long-term success. While some investors rely on instinct or speculation, the best approach is to use a structured, repeatable process that minimizes risk and maximizes returns. By following a streamlined four-step method, you can efficiently evaluate stocks and make informed decisions without spending hours analysing financial reports.

The first step in picking a great stock is to identify companies with a sustainable competitive advantage. A strong business moat ensures that a company can maintain its market position and protect itself from competitors.

Competitive advantages come in many forms, including brand strength, proprietary technology, cost leadership, and network effects. Companies like Apple, Microsoft, and Amazon have built dominant brands that allow them to retain customer loyalty and charge premium prices. Similarly, businesses with proprietary patents or exclusive technologies, such as pharmaceutical companies, have a natural advantage over competitors. A good stock is backed by a business that is difficult to disrupt and has a solid foundation for future growth.

Once you have identified a company with a solid market position, the next step is to evaluate its financial health. A business with weak financials, excessive debt, or declining revenues is a risky investment, regardless of how strong its brand might be. The best stocks are those with consistent revenue growth, strong profit margins, and manageable debt levels. Looking at a company's revenue and net income over the past five years can reveal whether it has a history of steady growth. High profit margins indicate pricing power, while low debt ensures that the company has financial flexibility. Companies with increasing free cash flow are especially attractive because they have money left over after expenses to reinvest in future growth, pay dividends, or reduce debt.

After confirming a company's financial strength, the next step is to determine whether the stock is priced. Even the best businesses can be poor investments if purchased at inflated prices. Many investors make the mistake of chasing hot stocks at their peaks, only to see them decline later. To avoid overpaying, you need to check valuation metrics like the Price-to-Earnings (P/E) ratio, Price-to-Book (P/B) ratio, and Price-to-Sales (P/S) ratio. Comparing these metrics to industry averages and the company's historical valuation can help determine whether a stock is trading at a reasonable price. Stocks with high valuation multiples relative to their historical averages or industry peers may be overvalued, while those with lower multiples could present attractive buying opportunities.

Even if a stock passes all previous tests, timing matters. Buying a great stock at the wrong time can result in short-term losses, even if the company is fundamentally strong. Many investors overlook the importance of market trends and technical indicators when making stock purchases. Checking support and resistance levels, moving averages, and overall market conditions can help identify the best time to enter a position. If a stock is trading near a support level or has recently bounced back from a correction, it may be a good entry point. Conversely, if the stock is at an all-time high with little room for further growth, it might be better to wait for a pullback before investing.

This entire process can be completed in just 15 minutes using free online tools like Yahoo Finance, Google Finance, and company earnings reports. By scanning a company's fundamentals, valuation, and technical indicators, you can quickly determine whether it is worth investing in or if you should move on to the next opportunity. The goal is to make decisions based on data, not emotions, and to invest in stocks with the best risk-reward profile.

Successful investing is not about predicting the future or finding the next Tesla or Amazon before anyone else. It is about consistently applying a structured approach to identify high-quality businesses that can grow over time. By following this 15-minute stock selection method, you can confidently build a portfolio of strong companies while avoiding the noise and speculation that often lead to poor investment decisions. The stock market rewards those who invest with discipline and patience, and by using this strategy, you will be well on your way to achieving financial success.

2.1 The 4-Step Formula for Finding Winning Stocks

Investing in the stock market is often perceived as a complex process requiring years of experience and deep financial knowledge. While expertise certainly plays a role in long-term success, the reality is that any investor can learn to pick winning stocks by following a structured, repeatable method. The key is to focus on the factors that truly determine a company's long-term success and avoid getting lost in irrelevant details or short-term market noise.

Many investors fall into the trap of making decisions based on emotions, media hype, or short-term trends. This leads to buying stocks at inflated prices, selling too soon, or investing in companies that lack strong fundamentals. The best approach is one that relies on data-driven analysis and a systematic selection process. This chapter introduces a 4-step formula designed to help investors efficiently evaluate stocks in just 15 minutes while ensuring that their investment decisions are based on sound financial principles.

Step 1: Identify Companies with a Strong Competitive Advantage

One of the most crucial factors in picking a winning stock is determining whether the company has a sustainable competitive advantage. A competitive advantage allows a company to maintain market leadership, protect its profits from competitors, and generate consistent returns for investors. Without this, even a profitable company can struggle to grow overall.

Competitive advantages come in different forms and understanding them is essential for selecting high-quality stocks. Some of the most significant types include:

- **Brand Power and Customer Loyalty** – Companies like Apple, Coca-Cola, and Nike have strong brand recognition that allows them to charge premium prices and retain loyal customers. Brand strength provides pricing power and demand stability.
- **Network Effects** – Businesses such as Meta (Facebook) and Visa benefit from network effects, meaning the more people who use their services, the more valuable they become. This creates a self-reinforcing cycle that strengthens their market position.
- **High Switching Costs** – Companies like Microsoft and Adobe provide software that becomes deeply embedded in their customers' operations, making it difficult or costly for users to switch to competitors.
- **Economies of Scale** – Amazon and Walmart leverage their vast scale to drive down costs, giving them a pricing advantage over smaller competitors.
- **Patents and Proprietary Technology** – Pharmaceutical companies like Pfizer and biotech firms benefit from patents that protect their innovations, ensuring they maintain a market advantage for years.

Identifying a company's competitive advantage is essential because it determines how well it can withstand market disruptions, economic downturns, and new competition. Companies that lack a strong competitive advantage often struggle to maintain profitability over the long term, making them less attractive investments.

Step 2: Evaluate Financial Strength and Stability

Even if a company has a dominant market position, it needs strong financials to be a worthwhile investment. A business with weak financials, excessive debt, or declining revenues can pose a significant risk, even if it operates in a promising industry. Investors should analyse key financial metrics to determine whether a company is financially sound.

Some of the most important financial indicators to assess include:

- **Revenue Growth** – A company should demonstrate consistent growth in revenue over several years. Revenue growth signals that demand for its products or services is increasing, which is essential for long-term value creation.
- **Profit Margins** – High and stable profit margins indicate pricing power, efficient operations, and strong demand. Companies with declining margins

may be facing increased costs or competitive pressures.

- **Earnings Per Share (EPS) and Net Income** – EPS measures a company's profitability on a per-share basis. Investors should look for companies with rising EPS and growing net income, as this indicates strong financial performance.
- **Return on Equity (ROE) and Return on Invested Capital (ROIC)** – ROE measures how efficiently a company generates profit from shareholders' equity, while ROIC indicates how effectively a business reinvests its earnings. A high ROE and ROIC suggest strong fiscal management.
- **Debt Levels (Debt-to-Equity Ratio)** – A financially healthy company should have manageable debt levels. Excessive debt can limit a company's ability to grow, reinvest in its business, or survive economic downturns.

Analysing these metrics allows investors to separate strong, financially stable companies from weaker ones. Companies that meet these criteria are more likely to withstand economic downturns, expand their operations, and provide consistent returns for shareholders.

Step 3: Assess Valuation to Avoid Overpaying

One of the most common mistakes investors make is buying great companies at the wrong price. Even the best businesses can become poor investments if purchased at excessively high valuations. This is why understanding valuation metrics is essential—it helps investors determine whether a stock is trading at a fair price or is overvalued.

Several valuation methods can help investors assess whether a stock is priced:

- **Price-to-Earnings (P/E) Ratio** – Compares a company's stock price to its earnings per share. A high P/E ratio may indicate overvaluation, while a low P/E ratio can signal an undervalued stock. Investors should compare the P/E ratio to industry averages and historical levels.
- **Price-to-Book (P/B) Ratio** – Compares the stock price to the company's book value. A lower P/B ratio suggests a stock may be undervalued.
- **Price-to-Sales (P/S) Ratio** – Measures a company's stock price relative to its revenue. A lower ratio often indicates a better value.

- **PEG Ratio (Price/Earnings-to-Growth)** – Adjusts the P/E ratio for expected earnings growth. A lower PEG ratio suggests a stock is attractively valued relative to its growth rate.

A stock's valuation should always be compared to its historical levels, competitors, and overall market conditions. Investors should avoid overpaying for hype-driven stocks and instead seek companies that are trading at reasonable or discounted valuations.

Step 4: Determine the Right Time to Buy

Even if a company has strong fundamentals and an attractive valuation, the timing of a purchase matters. Investors should avoid buying stocks based purely on emotions or speculation. Instead, understanding market trends and technical signals can improve decision-making.

Key factors to consider when timing a stock purchase include:

- **Support and Resistance Levels** – Support levels indicate a price where a stock tends to find buying interest, while resistance levels show where selling pressure often emerges. Buying near support levels can minimize downside risk.
- **Moving Averages (50-day and 200-day MA)** – Stocks that trade above their 50-day and 200-day moving averages often indicate upward momentum, while those below these levels may be in a downtrend.
- **Market Trends** – If the overall stock market is experiencing a downturn, even strong stocks can decline in price. Investors may want to wait for stabilization or signs of a recovery before making a purchase.

While long-term investors do not need to focus heavily on short-term market movements, buying at favourable price levels can improve returns and reduce risk.

Picking the best stocks does not require complex financial models or endless hours of research. By following a structured 4-step approach, investors can efficiently identify companies with strong competitive advantages, solid financials, reasonable valuations, and good entry points. This method removes the guesswork from stock selection and ensures that every investment decision is based on objective criteria rather than emotions or hype. Successful investing is about consistency and discipline. Rather than chasing the latest market trends, investors should focus on the fundamentals and apply a systematic approach to selecting stocks. By mastering this process, investors can build a high-quality portfolio and achieve long-term financial success.

2.2 How to Quickly Analyse a Company's Financial Health

Understanding a company's financial health is one of the most critical steps in stock investing. Even the most well-known brands can be poor investments if their financials are weak. Many investors focus too much on hype, news, or market trends, but the true strength of a company lies in its ability to generate consistent revenue, profits, and growth while managing debt responsibly.

This section provides a detailed framework for quickly assessing a company's financial health in a structured and efficient way. Instead of drowning in complex financial statements, investors should focus on the most critical metrics that determine whether a company is fundamentally strong. This approach allows investors to filter out weak companies quickly and focus on stocks with solid financial stability and long-term growth potential.

Step 1: Evaluating Revenue and Growth Trends

The first indicator of a company's financial health is its revenue growth. Revenue, also known as top-line growth, represents the total amount of money a company earns from its products or services before subtracting any costs or expenses. A growing revenue trend indicates that demand for the company's offerings is increasing, which is a positive sign for investors.

To analyse revenue effectively, investors should look at:

- **Year-over-Year (YoY) Revenue Growth** – These measures how much revenue has increased compared to the same period in the previous year. A consistent upward trend in revenue is a sign of a healthy company.
- **Quarter-over-Quarter (QoQ) Revenue Growth** – This shows how revenue is performing in recent quarters. Short-term fluctuations are normal, but a consistent decline over multiple quarters may indicate problems.

- **Five-Year Revenue Trend** – Looking at a company's revenue over a five-year period helps investors identify long-term growth patterns and avoid companies with unpredictable revenue streams.

A good example of revenue growth in action is companies like Amazon or Microsoft, which have shown consistent increases in revenue over the past decade. This signals strong demand and effective business execution. On the other hand, companies with stagnant or declining revenue may be struggling with competition, outdated products, or operational inefficiencies.

Step 2: Profitability – How Efficiently a Company Converts Revenue into Profit

Revenue alone is not enough—a company must be profitable to sustain growth and reward investors. Profitability measures how efficiently a company converts revenue into actual earnings after expenses, taxes, and costs.

The key profitability metrics investors should analyse are:

- **Net Income (Bottom Line)** – This represents the company's actual profit after all expenses are deducted. A rising net income over time is a sign of financial strength.
- **Earnings Per Share (EPS)** – EPS divides net income by the total number of outstanding shares, showing how much profit is generated for each share of stock. A growing EPS trend is a positive indicator.
- **Profit Margins (Gross, Operating, and Net Margins)** – These measure how efficiently a company turns revenue into profit. Companies with high margins have strong pricing power and cost management.
- **Gross Margin = (Revenue – Cost of Goods Sold) ÷ Revenue** – Indicates production efficiency.
- **Operating Margin = Operating Profit ÷ Revenue** – Measures core business profitability before taxes and interest.
- **Net Margin = Net Income ÷ Revenue** – Shows the company's overall profitability after all costs.

A company with rising profit margins is usually improving its efficiency, while declining margins could indicate rising costs, pricing pressure, or inefficient management.

For example, Apple has one of the highest profit margins in the technology sector, allowing it to generate massive profits despite competitive pricing pressures. In contrast, companies in industries with low margins, such as retail or airlines, may struggle with profitability due to prohibitive costs.

Step 3: Debt and Financial Stability – How Much Risk is Involved?

A company can have strong revenue and profitability, but if it carries too much debt, it becomes risky. Debt is necessary for business expansion, but excessive debt can limit a company's flexibility, increase financial stress, and even lead to bankruptcy in tough economic times.

Investors should focus on these key debt metrics:

- **Debt-to-Equity Ratio (D/E)** – Measures a company's debt relative to shareholder equity. A ratio below 1.0 is considered healthy, while a high ratio (above 2.0) may indicate excessive leverage.
- **Current Ratio and Quick Ratio** – These measure a company's ability to cover short-term obligations.
- **Current Ratio** = Current Assets ÷ Current Liabilities (A ratio above 1.5 is good.)
- **Quick Ratio** = (Current Assets – Inventory) ÷ Current Liabilities (A quick ratio above 1.0 is healthy.)
- **Interest Coverage Ratio** – Shows how easily a company can pay its interest expenses on outstanding debt. A ratio below 1.5 suggests potential financial trouble.

Companies with elevated levels of debt are more vulnerable during economic downturns. For example, many retail and airline companies struggled during the COVID-19 pandemic due to their high debt loads. In contrast, companies with low debt, such as Google (Alphabet), have greater financial flexibility and lower risk.

Step 4: Free Cash Flow – The Lifeline of a Business

Free cash flow (FCF) is one of the most important indicators of a company's financial health because it represents the cash a company has left after covering all expenses, including capital expenditures. FCF determines whether a company can invest in growth, return money to shareholders, or withstand economic downturns.

Positive Free Cash Flow – Indicates that a company generates excess cash beyond its operating needs, which can be reinvested in growth, dividends, or stock buybacks.

Negative Free Cash Flow – May indicate that a company is spending more than it earns, which could lead to financial difficulties unless it is in a high-growth phase.

Companies like Microsoft, Apple, and Visa generate massive free cash flow, which allows them to fund innovation, acquisitions, and shareholder returns. On the other hand, companies with consistent negative free cash flow may struggle with liquidity issues.

Putting It All Together – A Simple Process for Analysing Financial Health

By applying this structured approach, investors can quickly determine whether a company is financially strong or weak. Here is how to analyse any stock's financial health in five minutes:

- **Check Revenue Growth** – Look for consistent, increasing revenue over the past five years.
- **Analyse Profitability** – Examine EPS, net income, and profit margins to ensure the company is efficiently converting revenue into profit.
- **Assess Debt Levels** – Use the debt-to-equity ratio, current ratio, and interest coverage ratio to ensure the company is not overleveraged.
- **Review Free Cash Flow** – Ensure the company generates positive free cash flow, indicating it has enough cash to fund operations and growth.

If a company meets all four criteria, it is likely to be financially stable and a strong investment candidate. If it fails in one or more areas, further investigation is needed before making an investment decision.

Financial analysis does not have to be complicated. By focusing on revenue growth, profitability, debt levels, and free cash flow, investors can quickly determine whether a stock is a smart investment. The key to long-term success is to invest in companies with strong fundamentals, consistent growth, and responsible fiscal management.

Rather than relying on speculation or market trends, investors should base their decisions on data and objective financial analysis. A company with solid financial health is more likely to withstand economic downturns, expand its operations, and deliver strong returns over time.

By mastering these financial analysis techniques, investors can avoid risky stocks, identify winning companies, and build a high-quality investment portfolio with confidence.

2.3 The Key Metrics You Must Check Before Buying Any Stock

Investing in the stock market without analysing key financial metrics is like driving without checking the fuel gauge, speedometer, or warning lights. While stock prices fluctuate based on market sentiment, news, and macroeconomic conditions, a company's underlying financial metrics determine whether it is a strong investment or a potential disaster.

Many investors make the mistake of buying stocks based on hype, media recommendations, or gut feelings rather than looking at the numbers that reflect a company's strength. A stock may be popular, but that does not mean it is a worthwhile investment. To make informed decisions, investors must evaluate specific financial metrics that indicate profitability, stability, growth potential, and valuation.

This section outlines the key metrics every investor should analyse before buying a stock. These indicators provide a clear picture of a company's financial health, future potential, and whether the stock is trading at a reasonable price.

1. Revenue Growth – Is the Company Expanding?

Revenue, also known as top-line growth, represents the total sales a company generates from its products or services. A company that consistently grows revenue over time is expanding its market share, increasing demand, and successfully executing its business strategy.

When analysing revenue, consider:

- **Year-over-Year (YoY) Growth** – Compares revenue from the current year to the previous year. A steady increase is a positive sign, while declining revenue may indicate trouble.
- **Five-Year Revenue Trend** – Looking at long-term revenue trends prevents investors from being misled by short-term fluctuations.
- **Comparison to Industry Peers** – If a company's revenue is growing slower than its competitors, it may be losing market share.

For example, companies like Amazon and Microsoft have shown consistent revenue growth over the past decade, reflecting strong demand and solid business execution. In contrast, businesses with declining or stagnant revenue may be struggling with competition, poor management, or lack of innovation.

2. Earnings Per Share (EPS) – Is the Company Profitable?

Earnings Per Share (EPS) measures a company's profitability on a per-share basis. It tells investors how much profit the company generates for each outstanding share.

A consistently growing EPS indicates that the company is increasing its profitability, making it a potentially strong investment. Investors should compare:

- **Current EPS vs. Historical EPS** – A steady increase in EPS over time signals financial strength.
- **EPS vs. Analyst Expectations** – If a company consistently beats earnings estimates, it shows robust performance.
- **EPS Growth Rate** – Faster-growing EPS is a sign that the company is improving its profitability at a good pace.

Companies with strong and stable EPS growth, such as Apple and Google (Alphabet), tend to be strong long-term investments.

3. Profit Margins – How Efficient is the Company?

Profit margins measure how much of a company's revenue turns into actual profit. Companies with higher margins are more efficient, have better pricing power, and can manage cost increases without significantly affecting profitability.

Key profit margins to examine:

- **Gross Margin** – Measures how much profit remains after subtracting production costs. High gross margins indicate strong pricing power.
- **Operating Margin** – Shows how much profit remains after operating expenses (marketing, salaries, R&D).
- **Net Margin** – The final profitability indicator after all expenses, taxes, and interest are deducted.

A company with increasing profit margins is efficiently managing costs, while declining margins may signal rising expenses or pricing pressure.

For instance, Apple has some of the highest profit margins in the technology sector, allowing it to maintain strong profitability even with intense competition.

4. Return on Equity (ROE) and Return on Invested Capital (ROIC) – Is the Company Using Capital Wisely?

ROE and ROIC measure how efficiently a company generates profits from its investments and shareholders' equity.

Return on Equity (ROE) = Net Income ÷ Shareholder Equity

Return on Invested Capital (ROIC) = Net Operating Profit After Tax ÷ Total Capital Invested

A higher ROE or ROIC indicates that the company is using its capital effectively to generate returns for investors. Companies with strong ROE and ROIC, such as Microsoft and Visa, are known for high efficiency and excellent capital allocation.

A declining ROE or ROIC may indicate inefficient management, excessive debt, or declining profitability.

5. Debt-to-Equity Ratio – Is the Company Overleveraged?

Debt can be useful for expansion, but too much debt increases financial risk. The Debt-to-Equity (D/E) ratio measures how much debt a company has compared to its shareholder equity.

- **D/E Ratio Below 1.0** – A lower ratio indicates low financial risk and strong balance sheet stability.

- **D/E Ratio Above 2.0** – A high ratio may suggest the company is heavily reliant on debt, making it vulnerable during economic downturns.

Companies like Google (Alphabet) and Meta (Facebook) have low debt levels, making them financially stable even in uncertain market conditions. Conversely, companies with high debt loads, like airlines and retail chains, are more vulnerable during recessions.

6. Price-to-Earnings (P/E) Ratio – Is the Stock Overvalued or Undervalued?

The P/E ratio compares a stock's price to its earnings per share, helping investors determine whether a stock is expensive or priced.

- **Low P/E Ratio** – A stock may be undervalued, presenting a good buying opportunity.
- **High P/E Ratio** – The stock may be overvalued, meaning investors are paying a premium for future growth.
- Investors should compare the P/E ratio:

- **To its historical average** – A stock with a much higher P/E than its historical norm may be overvalued.
- **To industry peers** – A company with a significantly higher P/E than its competitors may be overpriced.

For example, Tesla has historically had a high P/E ratio, reflecting investor optimism about its future growth, while more stable companies like Procter & Gamble have lower, steady P/E ratios.

7. Free Cash Flow (FCF) – Does the Company Generate Cash?

Free Cash Flow (FCF) is one of the most important metrics for evaluating a company's financial strength. FCF represents the cash a company has left after covering all operating expenses and capital expenditures.

- **Positive Free Cash Flow** – The company has extra cash to invest in growth, pay dividends, or buy back shares.
- **Negative Free Cash Flow** – The company may be spending more than it earns, potentially leading to liquidity issues.

Companies like Microsoft, Apple, and Visa generate massive free cash flow, allowing them to fund innovation and return value to shareholders.

Putting It All Together – A Quick Checklist Before Buying a Stock

Before purchasing any stock, investors should go through this 7-metric checklist to ensure they are making a data-driven decision:

- **Revenue Growth** – Is the company growing consistently?
- **EPS Growth** – Is the company increasing profits per share?
- **Profit Margins** – Is the company efficient and maintaining strong margins?
- **ROE and ROIC** – Is the company effectively using capital?
- **Debt-to-Equity Ratio** – Does the company have manageable debt?
- **P/E Ratio** – Is the stock valued or overpriced?
- **Free Cash Flow** – Does the company generate strong cash flow?

If a stock meets all these criteria, it is likely to be a strong investment candidate. If it fails in multiple areas, further research is needed before deciding.

Analysing a stock before buying is essential for avoiding poor investments and maximizing returns. By focusing on these key metrics, investors can make informed, objective decisions rather than relying on emotions or market speculation. The stock market rewards those who invest in financially strong companies with sustainable growth and solid fundamentals.

Mastering these metrics will allow investors to build a high-quality portfolio, avoid common investment pitfalls, and achieve long-term financial success.

CHAPTER 3 – HOW TO KNOW IF A STOCK IS OVERVALUED OR UNDERVALUED

One of the biggest mistakes investors make is buying stocks at the wrong price. Even a great company can be a bad investment if purchased at an inflated valuation. The stock market operates on supply and demand, and stock prices fluctuate based on market sentiment, economic conditions, and speculation. However, the true value of a company is determined by its fundamentals and understanding how to assess whether a stock is overvalued or undervalued is a crucial skill for any investor.

Valuation is the process of determining how much a stock is worth relative to its earnings, assets, and growth potential. Investors who ignore valuation metrics often end up buying stocks at unsustainable highs, only to watch them decline when the hype fades. On the other hand, those who can identify undervalued stocks could buy strong businesses at a discount, maximizing their potential returns.

There are several ways to determine whether a stock is priced. The most common method is the price-to-earnings (P/E) ratio, which compares a company's stock price to its earnings per share. A high P/E ratio suggests that investors are paying a premium for future growth, while a low P/E ratio may indicate that the stock is undervalued. However, the P/E ratio should never be analysed in isolation. Comparing it to the company's historical P/E ratio, industry peers, and overall market conditions is essential to understanding whether a stock is terribly expensive or cheap.

Another critical metric is the price-to-book (P/B) ratio, which measures the stock's price relative to the company's book value, or the net value of its assets. A low P/B ratio can indicate that a stock is undervalued, particularly in industries with stable assets like banking or real estate. However, for high-growth companies, the P/B ratio may not be as relevant, since intangible assets such as brand value, intellectual property, and network effects are not fully captured in book value.

The price-to-sales (P/S) ratio is another tool that investors use to assess valuation. It compares the stock price to the company's total revenue. This metric is especially useful for evaluating growth companies that may not yet be profitable. A low P/S ratio suggests that the stock is trading at a low price compared to its revenue generation, which could indicate an undervaluation. However, the P/S ratio should always be analysed alongside profit margins, as a company with low profitability may not be a great investment even if its revenue is strong.

Another effective valuation method is the discounted cash flow (DCF) analysis, which estimates the present value of a company based on its expected future cash flows. This approach involves projecting the company's future earnings, discounting them to their present value using an appropriate discount rate, and comparing the result to the current stock price. While the DCF method is powerful, it requires making assumptions about future growth rates and interest rates, which introduces uncertainty.

Investors should also consider the PEG (price/earnings-to-growth) ratio, which adjusts the P/E ratio by factoring in the company's earnings growth rate. A stock with a high P/E but strong earnings growth may still be valued if its PEG ratio is low. A PEG ratio below 1 is considered a sign of undervaluation, while a PEG above 1.5 may indicate overvaluation.

Macroeconomic conditions also play a crucial role in stock valuation. Interest rates, inflation, and overall market sentiment can impact how stocks are priced. During periods of low interest rates, investors tend to pay higher valuations for growth stocks because future earnings are worth more in present terms. Conversely, in a high-interest-rate environment, valuation multiples often contract, as borrowing costs rise and investor appetite for risk decreases. Understanding how macroeconomic trends influence stock valuations can help investors make better decisions about when to buy or sell.

Market cycles also affect valuations. Stocks tend to be overvalued during market booms when optimism is high and undervalued during bear markets when fear dominates investor sentiment. Recognizing these patterns allows investors to take advantage of market inefficiencies. Contrarian investors often seek opportunities when stocks are trading below their intrinsic value due to temporary market pessimism. The famous strategy of buying when others are fearful and selling when others are greedy has been the foundation of many successful investors' portfolios.

Another important concept in valuation is margin of safety. Even if an investor believes a stock is undervalued, external factors such as unexpected earnings misses, economic downturns, or changes in industry trends can impact the company's performance. Buying a stock with a significant margin of safety— meaning it is trading well below its estimated intrinsic value—reduces the risk of loss. The larger the margin of safety, the less reliant an investor is on perfect market conditions for their investment to succeed.

Valuation should always be viewed in context. Some industries naturally have higher valuation multiples than others. Technology companies, for example, often trade at higher P/E ratios due to their robust growth potential, while utility stocks typically have lower valuations because of their stable, predictable earnings. Comparing a company's valuation to its industry peers is essential for determining whether it is truly overvalued or undervalued.

Investors should also pay attention to forward-looking metrics rather than just historical data. Forward P/E ratios, analyst earnings estimates, and projected revenue growth provide insight into how a company is expected to perform in the future. Stocks that appear expensive based on historical valuation metrics may still be good investments if their growth prospects are strong.

One of the most valuable skills an investor can develop is patience. Many investors rush to buy stocks without considering valuation, fearing they will miss gains. However, disciplined investors wait for the right price, allowing them to enter at levels that provide strong long-term returns. The best opportunities often arise when high-quality stocks are temporarily mispriced due to short-term market fluctuations.

Understanding whether a stock is overvalued or undervalued is not about finding a single perfect metric but about combining multiple valuation tools to form a complete picture. No valuation method is foolproof, but using a combination of P/E, P/B, P/S, PEG, and DCF analysis, along with a strong understanding of macroeconomic conditions and market sentiment, allows investors to make informed decisions.

Successful investing is not about buying stocks at any price but about purchasing great companies at reasonable valuations. Investors who focus on valuation, rather than speculation, build portfolios that stand the test of time, delivering consistent returns while minimizing risk. Mastering the art of stock valuation allows investors to confidently navigate market fluctuations, avoid overpriced assets, and capitalize on undervalued opportunities, leading to long-term financial success.

3.1 Warren Buffett's Strategy for Finding Fairly Priced Stocks

Warren Buffett, widely regarded as one of the greatest investors of all time, has built his fortune by following a disciplined approach to stock selection. Unlike traders who focus on short-term price movements, Buffett's strategy is rooted in fundamental analysis, intrinsic value assessment, and long-term investing. His ability to find priced stocks with strong business fundamentals has led to decades of exceptional returns. Understanding his strategy provides investors with a reliable framework for identifying undervalued stocks and avoiding overhyped investments.

Buffett's investment philosophy is guided by value investing, a method pioneered by his mentor Benjamin Graham. The core principle of value investing is to buy stocks at a price lower than their intrinsic value, ensuring a margin of safety. While many investors chase high-growth companies regardless of their valuations, Buffett believes that a great company is only a worthwhile investment if purchased at a reasonable price. His strategy focuses on business quality, financial strength, competitive advantages, and rational pricing.

The first step in Buffett's strategy is identifying businesses with a durable competitive advantage. He refers to this as an economic moat, a characteristic that protects a company from competitors and allows it to maintain profitability over time. Companies with strong brands, proprietary technology, cost leadership, or high customer retention tend to outperform their rivals. For example, Coca-Cola's global brand power, Apple's ecosystem of interconnected products, and Visa's dominant payment network give them sustainable advantages that competitors find difficult to replicate. Buffett avoids industries with low barriers to entry or companies that rely on temporary trends, as these businesses are more vulnerable to disruption.

Once a company with a durable competitive advantage is identified, the next step is assessing its financial strength. Buffett prioritizes companies with consistent revenue and earnings growth, stable profit margins, and low debt levels. He carefully examines financial statements to ensure that a business is generating strong cash flow and reinvesting profits efficiently. Key financial metrics that Buffett uses include return on equity (ROE), return on invested capital (ROIC), and free cash flow (FCF). A high ROE indicates that the company is effectively using shareholder capital to generate profits, while strong ROIC shows that management is making smart investment decisions.

One of Buffett's key principles is avoiding excessive debt. Companies with high debt levels are more vulnerable during economic downturns, as they must continue making interest payments regardless of revenue fluctuations. Buffett prefers businesses with manageable debt-to-equity ratios, allowing them to navigate economic uncertainty without financial distress. He also looks at the interest coverage ratio, which measures how easily a company can pay its debt obligations. If a company's earnings are barely sufficient to cover interest expenses, it is considered too risky for investment.

The next critical step in Buffett's strategy is determining the intrinsic value of a stock. Instead of relying solely on market prices, Buffett calculates a company's true worth based on its future earnings potential. One of his preferred valuation methods is the discounted cash flow (DCF) model, which estimates the present value of a company's future cash flows. By discounting expected earnings to their present value using an appropriate discount rate, Buffett determines whether a stock is trading below its intrinsic value. If the stock's current market price is significantly lower than its intrinsic value, it presents a buying opportunity.

Buffett also considers price-to-earnings (P/E) ratios, price-to-book (P/B) ratios, and free cash flow yield when evaluating stock valuations. However, he does not rely on these metrics alone, as they can sometimes be misleading. Instead, he compares them to industry peers and historical averages to assess whether a stock is priced. Buffett believes that a great company can be a terrible investment if purchased at an excessively high valuation, which is why he remains patient and waits for the right buying opportunity.

Another fundamental aspect of Buffett's strategy is investing with a long-term perspective. He famously said, "Our favourite holding period is forever," emphasizing his belief in owning strong businesses for decades rather than trading frequently. Short-term market fluctuations do not concern him; instead, he focuses on a company's ability to grow earnings consistently over time. This long-term mindset allows him to benefit from the power of compound growth, which has been a cornerstone of his investment success.

Buffett also emphasizes management quality as a crucial factor in investment decisions. He looks for companies with competent, shareholder-friendly leadership that prioritizes sustainable growth over short-term profits. He values businesses where executives have a track record of efficient capital allocation, ethical decision-making, and clear long-term vision. One of his preferred indicators is insider ownership, which shows whether company executives have significant personal stakes in the company. High insider ownership aligns management's interests with shareholders, as executives are incentivized to drive long-term value.

A critical component of Buffett's investment philosophy is avoiding speculative investments. He has famously avoided technology stocks for most of his career, not because they lack growth potential, but because he does not invest in businesses he does not fully understand. He believes that investors should stay within their circle of competence, meaning they should focus on industries and companies they have deep knowledge of. This approach prevents unnecessary risks and ensures well-informed investment decisions.

Buffett's strategy also includes ignoring market noise and focusing on fundamentals. He does not react to short-term market movements, media headlines, or economic forecasts. Instead, he remains committed to his investment principles, knowing that stock prices fluctuate in the short term but reflect a company's true value overall. This disciplined approach allows him to buy undervalued stocks when the market overreacts to temporary setbacks and hold onto strong businesses through periods of volatility.

One of the most valuable lessons from Buffett is the importance of patience. Many investors feel the need to be constantly active in the market, but Buffett believes that waiting for the right investment opportunity is more important than frequent trading. He compares investing to a baseball game, where there are no called strikes, meaning an investor can wait for the perfect pitch before swinging. This mindset prevents impulsive decisions and ensures that every investment is made with conviction.

Buffett also follows the margin of safety principle, which means only investing when a stock's price is significantly below its intrinsic value. This approach minimizes downside risk and provides a buffer in case future earnings do not meet expectations. By buying stocks with a margin of safety, investors reduce the likelihood of significant losses and increase their chances of achieving strong long-term returns.

Applying Buffett's strategy requires discipline, patience, and a focus on long-term value creation. His method is not about chasing quick profits but about identifying great businesses at reasonable prices and holding them for years, if not decades. Investors who adopt this approach benefit from steady compounding growth, reduced risk, and greater financial security.

Understanding and implementing Warren Buffett's strategy provides investors with a proven framework for identifying priced stocks. By focusing on business quality, financial strength, intrinsic value, and long-term investing, investors can build a portfolio that withstands market fluctuations and delivers sustainable returns. Mastering this approach is not about finding the next big trend but about consistently investing in high-quality businesses with strong fundamentals at reasonable valuations.

3.2 How to Use the P/E Ratio and Other Valuation Indicators

Valuing a stock correctly is one of the most important skills an investor can develop. A company may have strong financials and a competitive advantage, but if its stock is overpriced, it may not be a worthwhile investment. Conversely, some companies trade below their true value, presenting great buying opportunities. To determine whether a stock is valued, investors rely on several key valuation metrics, the most common being the Price-to-Earnings (P/E) ratio. However, P/E alone is not enough, and a deeper analysis using other valuation indicators provides a more accurate assessment of whether a stock is overvalued, undervalued, or fairly priced.

The P/E ratio is one of the simplest and most widely used valuation tools in investing. It measures how much investors are willing to pay for each dollar of earnings generated by a company. The formula for calculating the P/E ratio is:

$$P/E = \frac{\text{Stock Price}}{\text{Earnings Per Share (EPS)}}$$

A high P/E ratio suggests that investors expect strong future growth, as they are willing to pay a premium for the stock. A low P/E ratio, on the other hand, may indicate that the stock is undervalued or that investors have low expectations for its future performance. However, P/E ratios must always be interpreted in context. A company with a high P/E ratio is not necessarily overpriced, just as a company with a low P/E is not always a bargain. Comparing a company's P/E ratio to its historical levels, industry peers, and the overall market provides a clearer picture of its valuation.

Investors distinguish between trailing P/E and forward P/E. The trailing P/E is based on a company's past 12 months of earnings, while the forward P/E uses projected future earnings. The forward P/E is particularly useful in assessing growth companies because it accounts for expected earnings increases. If a stock's forward P/E is significantly lower than its trailing P/E, it may indicate that earnings are expected to grow, making the stock a better value than it appears at first glance.

While the P/E ratio is useful, it has limitations. It does not account for debt, cash flow, or a company's overall financial health. Some industries naturally have higher or lower P/E ratios. For example, technology and high-growth companies typically have higher P/E ratios because investors expect substantial future earnings growth. In contrast, utility or consumer staple stocks often have lower P/E ratios due to their stable but slow growth patterns. Comparing a company's P/E to others in the same industry is essential for making a fair assessment.

Another valuable valuation metric is the Price-to-Book (P/B) ratio, which compares a company's market price to its book value. Book value represents the net value of a company's assets, making the P/B ratio useful for assessing whether a stock is trading below its actual worth. The formula for the P/B ratio is:

$$P/B = \frac{\text{Stock Price}}{\text{Book Value Per Share}}$$

A P/B ratio below 1.0 suggests that a stock is undervalued because the market price is lower than the company's asset value. However, this metric is more relevant for asset-heavy industries such as banking, manufacturing, and real estate. Companies with significant intangible assets, like brand reputation or intellectual property, may have a high P/B ratio but still be valued.

The Price-to-Sales (P/S) ratio is another useful indicator, especially for companies that are not yet profitable. It compares a company's market capitalization to its total revenue. The formula is:

$$P/S = \frac{\text{Market Capitalization}}{\text{Total Revenue}}$$

A low P/S ratio suggests that investors are paying less for each dollar of revenue, which can indicate undervaluation. However, this metric does not consider profitability, so it should be used alongside earnings and cash flow analysis.

Another advanced valuation metric is the Price/Earnings-to-Growth (PEG) ratio, which refines the P/E ratio by factoring in a company's earnings growth rate. The formula for the PEG ratio is:

$$PEG = \frac{P/E}{\text{Earnings Growth Rate}}$$

A PEG ratio below 1.0 is considered a sign that a stock is undervalued relative to its growth potential. If a company has a high P/E ratio but also a high growth rate, its PEG ratio might still indicate that it is a worthwhile investment. This metric is particularly useful for evaluating high-growth stocks, as it balances valuation with future potential.

Another critical valuation tool is Enterprise Value-to-EBITDA (EV/EBITDA), which measures a company's total value relative to its earnings before interest, taxes, depreciation, and amortization (EBITDA). **The formula is:**

$$EV/EBITDA = \frac{\text{Enterprise Value}}{\text{EBITDA}}$$

Enterprise value (EV) includes market capitalization, debt, and cash, providing a more comprehensive valuation than market cap alone. A low EV/EBITDA ratio indicates that a stock is trading at a discount compared to its earnings potential. This metric is particularly useful for comparing companies with different capital structures, as it accounts for debt levels.

Another method for assessing valuation is the Discounted Cash Flow (DCF) model, which calculates the present value of a company's future cash flows. This method requires making assumptions about future revenue, expenses, and discount rates, making it more complex than simple valuation ratios. However, it is one of the most powerful tools for estimating a stock's true worth. If the DCF valuation is significantly higher than the current stock price, it suggests that the stock is undervalued.

Understanding valuation metrics is only part of the equation. Investors must also consider market sentiment, macroeconomic conditions, and industry trends. Stocks can remain undervalued for extended periods if investors are pessimistic about an industry or if broader market conditions are unfavourable. Similarly, overvalued stocks can continue rising due to publicise and speculation. This is why valuation should always be combined with fundamental and technical analysis for a complete investment picture.

A key principle in valuation is the margin of safety. Even when a stock appears to be valued based on fundamental metrics, external factors such as economic downturns, industry disruptions, or changes in leadership can impact its performance. Buying a stock at a price significantly below its estimated intrinsic value provides a cushion against unexpected risks. This principle, popularized by Benjamin Graham and followed by Warren Buffett, helps investors protect their capital while maximizing potential gains.

Investors should also recognize that valuation metrics have limitations. Some industries, such as high-growth technology companies, often trade at high P/E ratios for extended periods because of their future earnings potential. On the other hand, some undervalued stocks remain cheap because they face fundamental business challenges that prevent growth. This is why valuation should never be the sole factor in an investment decision—a stock's financial health, competitive position, and long-term prospects are equally important.

The ability to determine whether a stock is overvalued, undervalued, or fairly priced is an essential skill for building a successful investment portfolio. While the P/E ratio is a useful starting point, combining it with P/B, P/S, PEG, EV/EBITDA, and DCF analysis provides a more complete valuation picture. By understanding and applying these valuation metrics correctly, investors can avoid overpriced stocks, identify hidden opportunities, and make data-driven decisions.

Mastering valuation is not about predicting short-term price movements but about ensuring that every investment is made with a rational and disciplined approach. Investors who focus on valuation alongside strong business fundamentals have a higher likelihood of achieving consistent long-term returns, minimizing risk, and building a portfolio that withstands market fluctuations.

3.3 The Biggest Mistake: Why Buying Cheap Stocks Can Be a Trap

Many investors believe that buying low-priced stocks automatically means they are getting a bargain. The logic seems simple: if a stock is trading at a low price compared to its past levels, it must be a good deal. However, this mindset can be one of the most dangerous mistakes in investing. A cheap stock is not always a good stock, and in many cases, a low price can signal deeper issues within the company. Understanding why some stocks trade at low valuations—and whether they present an opportunity or a trap—is essential to avoiding costly mistakes.

One of the most common misconceptions is that a low share price means a stock is undervalued. Investors often assume that a company trading at $5 per share is cheaper than one trading at $200 per share. However, a stock's price alone tells nothing about its value. What truly matters is the company's market capitalization —the total value of all outstanding shares. A stock with a low share price can still be overvalued if its earnings and growth potential are weak. Conversely, a high-priced stock can be a great investment if the company has strong financials and long-term potential.

The biggest danger of buying cheap stocks is the risk of value traps. A value trap occurs when a stock appears undervalued based on traditional valuation metrics such as the price-to-earnings (P/E) ratio, price-to-book (P/B) ratio, or price-to-sales (P/S) ratio, but the underlying business is deteriorating. Investors who focus solely on low valuation ratios without examining the company's fundamentals may find themselves stuck in stocks that continue to decline in value.

There are several reasons why a stock may be cheap, and distinguishing between temporary setbacks and long-term structural problems is crucial. Some stocks trade at low prices because of short-term market overreactions—a company may have missed earnings expectations, experienced negative press, or suffered from broader market downturns. In these cases, if the company's fundamentals remain strong, the stock may present a buying opportunity. However, in many cases, stocks are cheap because of fundamental weaknesses, such as declining revenue, high debt, poor management, or structural declines in the industry.

A classic example of a value trap is companies in declining industries. Businesses that once dominated their markets can become obsolete due to technological advancements, changing consumer preferences, or stronger competition. Traditional retail stores, print media companies, and coal energy producers are examples of industries that have seen long-term declines. A stock in a dying industry may trade at what looks like a bargain price, but if the company's business model is failing, the stock price may continue to fall indefinitely.

High debt levels are another major red flag when evaluating cheap stocks. A company with excessive debt is vulnerable to financial distress, particularly in times of economic downturns or rising interest rates. If earnings are not sufficient to cover debt payments, the company may be forced to issue new shares, dilute existing shareholders, or even file for bankruptcy. Investors often underestimate the risks associated with debt-heavy companies trading at low valuations. Just because a stock has fallen significantly does not mean it will recover—if a company is burdened by debt, its stock price can continue declining until it becomes worthless.

Earnings deterioration is another warning sign that a cheap stock may not be a worthwhile investment. A declining P/E ratio does not always indicate a bargain; it can also signal shrinking profitability. If a company's earnings are in a long-term decline, even a low stock price may not be enough to justify an investment. This is particularly dangerous in cyclical industries, where companies experience periods of boom and bust. Stocks in industries such as oil, commodities, and manufacturing can appear cheap at the peak of an economic cycle but continue to decline as demand weakens.

Investors should also be cautious of penny stocks, which are stocks trading at exceptionally low prices, often under $5 per share. Penny stocks are highly speculative, often belonging to small or struggling companies with uncertain futures. These stocks are prone to manipulation, low liquidity, and extreme volatility. Many inexperienced investors are attracted to penny stocks because they believe they can generate huge returns with small investments. However, the reality is that most penny stocks fail, and investors lose their money.

Another common pitfall is overreliance on past stock performance. Investors often assume that a stock that once traded at $50 but is now priced at $10 is guaranteed to return to its previous highs. However, stock prices do not have a natural tendency to "return" to previous levels unless the company's fundamentals justify it. A stock that has fallen significantly is often a sign of underlying business problems, and without strong catalysts for recovery, it may continue declining.

A better approach to identifying undervalued stocks is to focus on quality companies with strong fundamentals that are temporarily mispriced by the market. Instead of buying stocks just because they are cheap, investors should look for businesses with growing revenue, strong profit margins, manageable debt, and a durable competitive advantage. Companies that have experienced short-term price declines due to external factors, such as temporary economic downturns or market corrections, may present attractive buying opportunities—but only if their long-term business prospects remain strong.

To avoid falling into value traps, investors should conduct thorough research beyond basic valuation ratios. Looking at a company's earnings growth trends, cash flow stability, industry outlook, and competitive positioning can help separate genuine bargains from stocks that are cheap for a reason. Analysing management effectiveness, checking whether insiders are buying or selling shares, and reviewing the company's historical financial performance provide additional insights.

Another useful strategy is comparing a company's valuation to historical levels and industry benchmarks. If a stock is trading at a lower P/E or P/B ratio than its historical average but its fundamentals remain solid, it may be undervalued. However, if the entire industry is experiencing declining valuations due to changing market conditions, the stock may not be as attractive as it seems. Investors should also consider macroeconomic factors such as interest rates, inflation, and consumer spending trends, which can impact valuations across different sectors.

A disciplined approach to investing involves recognizing that not all low-priced stocks are opportunities. The best investments come from buying strong businesses at fair prices, not weak businesses at cheap prices. A stock trading at an attractive valuation should still be evaluated for growth potential, competitive position, financial health, and future earnings stability. Patience and thorough analysis help investors avoid stocks that continue to decline and instead focus on companies with strong fundamentals that are temporarily undervalued.

In investing, cheap is not always good, and expensive is not always bad. Some high-priced stocks continue to rise because they belong to companies with exceptional business models and strong prospects. Likewise, some low-priced stocks remain stagnant or continue falling due to structural weaknesses. The key to successful investing is identifying stocks that are priced relative to their true intrinsic value rather than simply looking for low prices.

By understanding why stocks become undervalued and applying a rigorous selection process, investors can avoid the pitfalls of value traps, penny stocks, and debt-heavy companies. Instead of chasing low-priced stocks hoping for a rebound, investors should focus on quality businesses with solid long-term potential, ensuring a higher probability of consistent returns and reduced investment risk

CHAPTER 4 – WHEN TO BUY AND WHEN TO SELL A STOCK

One of the biggest challenges in investing is deciding when to buy and when to sell a stock. Many investors focus on picking the right companies but fail to recognize the importance of timing their entries and exits. Even the best stock can lead to losses if purchased at an inflated price, while a poorly timed sale can result in missed opportunities for significant gains. Understanding the factors that influence stock movements, valuations, and investor sentiment is critical to maximizing returns and minimizing risk.

Buying a stock should never be based on speculation, hype, or emotional reactions to market trends. Instead, investors should follow a structured approach that considers fundamental analysis, valuation, and market timing. The most crucial factor in determining when to buy a stock is ensuring that the underlying company is financially strong and has sustainable growth potential. A company should have consistent revenue and earnings growth, strong profit margins, a durable competitive advantage, and a healthy balance sheet. Stocks that meet these criteria are more likely to generate long-term returns, while companies with declining financials or excessive debt pose greater risks.

Even if a company is fundamentally strong, its stock price must also be fairly valued before making a purchase. Many investors overpay for stocks due to market hype, only to see their investments decline when the excitement fades. Valuation metrics such as the price-to-earnings (P/E) ratio, price-to-book (P/B) ratio, price-to-sales (P/S) ratio, and discounted cash flow (DCF) analysis help determine whether a stock is overvalued or trading at a reasonable price. Comparing these metrics to historical averages, industry peers, and overall market conditions provides a clearer picture of whether the stock presents a buying opportunity or a potential risk.

Market conditions also play a key role in determining the best time to buy a stock. Broad market trends, economic cycles, and investor sentiment influence stock prices. Stocks tend to perform better in bull markets, where investor confidence is high and economic conditions are favourable, while prices often decline in bear markets due to uncertainty and pessimism. Buying during market corrections or periods of fear can provide investors with better entry points, as many high-quality stocks temporarily trade at discounted prices. However, it is essential to differentiate between a temporary dip and a long-term decline caused by fundamental weaknesses in a company or industry.

Another important consideration when timing stock purchases is technical analysis, which involves studying price trends, support, and resistance levels, and moving averages. While long-term investors primarily focus on fundamentals, technical indicators can help refine entry points. For example, buying a stock near a historical support level can reduce downside risk, while avoiding stocks that have recently surged to all-time highs can prevent overpaying. The 50-day and 200-day moving averages can also provide insight into whether a stock is in an uptrend or downtrend, guiding investors on when to initiate a position.

Once an investor has purchased a stock, the next challenge is knowing when to sell. Selling too early can result in missing future gains, while holding onto a stock for too long can lead to unnecessary losses. A well-defined exit strategy is essential to managing risk and maximizing profits. The most important reason to sell a stock is when its fundamentals deteriorate. If a company experiences declining revenue, shrinking profit margins, excessive debt accumulation, or weakening competitive position, it may no longer be a strong investment. Investors should closely monitor quarterly earnings reports, industry trends, and company management decisions to assess whether the original investment thesis remains intact.

Another reason to sell is when a stock becomes significantly overvalued. If a stock's valuation reaches historically elevated levels relative to earnings and industry benchmarks, it may indicate that the price has outpaced its growth potential. Holding onto overvalued stocks increases the risk of future corrections, and selling at peak valuations allows investors to lock in profits before a potential downturn. While it is difficult to predict exact market tops, comparing a stock's current valuation metrics to historical trends can help determine whether it is time to take profits.

Portfolio rebalancing is another reason investors may need to sell stocks. Over time, certain stocks may outperform and become an oversized portion of a portfolio, increasing overall risk exposure. Selling a portion of overperforming stocks and reallocating funds into undervalued opportunities ensures that the portfolio remains diversified and balanced. This strategy helps mitigate risk while maintaining exposure to high-growth investments.

Investors should also consider selling stocks when better opportunities arise. Capital in the stock market should always be allocated to the best risk-reward opportunities. If a stock no longer presents strong upside potential or a better investment opportunity becomes available, selling and reinvesting in a higher-quality stock can improve long-term returns. However, investors should avoid frequent trading, as excessive buying and selling can lead to increased transaction costs and reduced compounding benefits.

A common mistake investor make is holding onto losing stocks in the hope of recovery, even when fundamentals suggest otherwise. This psychological bias, known as the sunk cost fallacy, leads investors to keep bad investments instead of reallocating their money into stronger opportunities. If a stock's long-term outlook has deteriorated, it is often better to sell and move on rather than waiting for a turnaround that may never happen.

Market sentiment and macroeconomic conditions can also signal when it is time to reduce stock exposure. During periods of rising interest rates, high inflation, or economic uncertainty, certain sectors may underperform, making it beneficial to shift investments into more defensive assets such as consumer staples, healthcare, or dividend-paying stocks. Investors should remain aware of broader economic trends that could impact the performance of specific industries or market sectors.

One of the most important aspects of selling stocks is avoiding emotional decision-making. Many investors panic during market downturns and sell stocks out of fear, only to watch them rebound shortly after. On the other hand, some investors refuse to sell winning stocks due to greed, hoping for even higher returns, only to see gains erased when a market correction occurs. A disciplined approach, based on rational analysis rather than emotions, leads to better long-term outcomes.

Successful investing requires both patience and decisiveness. Knowing when to buy and sell stocks is not about making perfect predictions but about following a structured process that minimizes risk and maximizes returns. Buying fundamentally strong companies at reasonable valuations, selling when fundamentals weaken or valuations become excessive, and maintaining a disciplined approach to portfolio management allows investors to navigate market fluctuations effectively.

Mastering the timing of stock purchases and sales is a skill that improves with experience. Investors who develop a clear strategy based on fundamental analysis, valuation metrics, and market conditions will be better positioned to make confident decisions, avoid common pitfalls, and build long-term wealth through strategic investing.

4.1 The Psychology of Buying and Selling Stocks: How to Avoid Emotional Mistakes

One of the most overlooked yet critical aspects of investing is psychology. The stock market is driven not only by financial fundamentals but also by human emotions such as fear, greed, overconfidence, and panic. Many investors make irrational decisions when buying and selling stocks because they allow emotions to dictate their actions rather than following a logical and disciplined approach. Understanding the psychological traps that lead to poor decision-making and developing strategies to control emotions can significantly improve investment outcomes and long-term returns.

A common mistake investor makes when buying stocks is chasing trends and hype. When a stock is rapidly increasing in price, the fear of missing out (FOMO) often pushes investors to buy without rigorously evaluating the company's fundamentals. This behaviour leads to purchasing stocks at inflated prices, only to watch them decline once the excitement fades. Many investors rush into stocks that have already seen massive gains, believing they will continue to rise indefinitely. However, history has repeatedly shown that parabolic price movements are unsustainable, and stocks that soar due to hype often experience sharp corrections when market sentiment shifts. The best way to avoid this trap is to ignore short-term market noise and focus on companies with strong financials, reasonable valuations, and long-term growth potential.

Another major psychological trap when buying stocks is confirmation bias, which occurs when investors selectively seek information that supports their pre-existing beliefs while ignoring contradictory evidence. Once an investor becomes convinced that a stock is a great investment, they may dismiss warning signs such as slowing revenue growth, rising debt levels, or increasing competition. This bias leads to overconfidence, causing investors to underestimate risks and make impulsive decisions. The best way to combat confirmation bias is to approach investing with an open mind by actively looking for reasons not to buy a stock. Challenging one's assumptions and considering alternative viewpoints helps investors make more balanced decisions.

The disposition effect is another common psychological mistake, which refers to the tendency of investors to sell winning stocks too early while holding onto losing stocks too long. Many investors panic when a stock they own starts declining in price, fearing further losses, and they sell out of fear instead of evaluating whether the company's long-term fundamentals remain strong. Conversely, when a stock is performing well, some investors sell too soon to "lock in profits" instead of allowing their investments to grow. This behaviour stems from loss aversion, the idea that people feel the pain of losses more intensely than the pleasure of equivalent gains. Successful investors overcome this bias by sticking to a clear investment thesis—if a company remains fundamentally strong, short-term price fluctuations should not dictate selling decisions.

One of the most destructive psychological traps is anchoring bias, where investors fixate on past stock prices and use them as reference points for decision-making. If a stock was trading at $100 six months ago and is now at $50, many investors assume that it is a great buying opportunity simply because it is cheaper than before. However, a lower price does not necessarily mean a stock is undervalued—there may be fundamental reasons why its price has declined, such as declining sales, loss of market share, or mismanagement. Instead of anchoring to past prices, investors should assess whether the company's future potential justifies its current valuation.

Overtrading is another psychological pitfall that negatively impacts returns. Many investors believe that constantly buying and selling stocks will maximize profits, but frequent trading leads to higher transaction costs, tax inefficiencies, and increased stress. Overtrading is often driven by the illusion of control, where investors feel they must always "do something" to stay ahead of the market. The best investors recognize that patience is a powerful tool—holding onto great stocks for the long term and avoiding unnecessary trades allows compounding to work in their Favor. Instead of trying to time every small market movement, investors should focus on long-term wealth creation by owning high-quality businesses.

Market crashes and corrections test investors' emotional discipline more than anything else. During times of extreme market volatility, panic sets in, and many investors sell their stocks out of fear that prices will continue to decline. However, history has shown that selling during a downturn often leads to regret, as markets tend to recover over time. Investors who sell out of fear often end up buying back at higher prices when optimism returns, which locks in losses and reduces overall returns. The best way to manage market downturns is to stay focused on long-term goals, maintain a diversified portfolio, and use downturns as opportunities to buy great companies at discounted prices. Instead of reacting emotionally to short-term declines, investors should view corrections as buying opportunities for stocks they believe in.

Behavioural finance studies have shown that most investors underperform the market because of poor decision-making caused by emotions. Research from Dalbar, a financial analytics firm, has consistently found that the average investor achieves significantly lower returns than the broader market index due to mistimed entries and exits. Investors who chase performance, panic sell, and make frequent trades often erode their gains. The key to overcoming these challenges is developing a systematic investment process that removes emotion from decision-making. This can include creating a written investment plan, setting clear buy and sell criteria, and regularly reviewing holdings based on objective financial metrics rather than market sentiment.

Having a long-term mindset is one of the most effective ways to counteract emotional biases. Legendary investors such as Warren Buffett emphasize that successful investing is about patience, discipline, and rationality, not short-term speculation. Buffett has famously said, "The stock market is a device for transferring money from the impatient to the patient." Instead of constantly reacting to short-term price movements, successful investors focus on owning high-quality businesses that can grow over time.

A useful strategy for managing emotions in investing is recommitting to a decision-making framework. Before buying a stock, investors should define their investment thesis, price target, and exit strategy. This prevents them from making impulsive decisions based on fear or greed. For example, if an investor buys a stock expecting it to grow earnings at 10% per year, they should only consider selling if the company's earnings growth slows significantly, the industry landscape changes, or the valuation becomes excessive. Setting predefined stop-loss levels can also help mitigate risk without requiring emotionally driven decisions.

Mindfulness and self-awareness play a significant role in improving investment outcomes. Investors who recognize their own behavioural tendencies—whether they are prone to fear, greed, or overconfidence—can take steps to counteract their biases. Keeping an investment journal where investors document their reasons for buying or selling a stock can provide valuable insights into their decision-making process over time. Reviewing past trades and analysing whether they were based on sound logic or emotions helps improve future investment discipline.

Mastering the psychology of buying and selling stocks is just as important as understanding financial statements or valuation metrics. The ability to control emotions, think independently, and make rational decisions separates successful investors from those who fall victim to market fluctuations. By recognizing and overcoming psychological biases such as FOMO, confirmation bias, the disposition effect, anchoring, overtrading, and panic selling, investors can develop a disciplined approach to investing that leads to long-term success. A well-defined investment strategy that prioritizes rational decision-making over emotional reactions allows investors to maximize returns, minimize mistakes, and achieve financial security in the stock market.

4.2 How to Identify Market Tops and Bottoms: A Strategic Approach to Timing

Understanding when a market or individual stock has reached its peak or bottom is one of the most valuable skills an investor can develop. While no one can predict market movements with absolute certainty, certain indicators and patterns consistently signal overvaluation or undervaluation, helping investors make better buying and selling decisions. Market tops and bottoms are driven by a combination of economic cycles, investor sentiment, technical indicators, and fundamental factors, all of which provide clues about whether it is time to buy, hold, or sell.

A market top occurs when stock prices reach their peak before a decline begins. These periods are often characterized by extreme optimism, speculative excess, and inflated valuations. The psychological factor at play during a market top is euphoria —investors become overly confident, believing that stocks will continue rising indefinitely. This leads to reckless behaviour, including buying stocks at unsustainable prices, excessive use of leverage, and ignoring warning signs of an impending downturn. A classic example of this was the dot-com bubble of the late 1990s, when technology stocks soared to astronomical levels despite many companies having little to no profits. Similarly, in the housing market bubble of 2008, investors continued buying properties at inflated prices under the belief that housing values would never decline.

One of the most reliable signs of a market top is excessive valuations. When price-to-earnings (P/E) ratios, price-to-book (P/B) ratios, and price-to-sales (P/S) ratios become significantly higher than historical averages, it often suggests that stocks are overvalued. Comparing current valuation metrics to long-term trends can help investors identify whether a market is in bubble territory. Another red flag is parabolic price increases, where stocks or entire markets experience rapid gains in a brief period. While strong uptrends are common in bull markets, price movements that become unsustainable often indicate speculation rather than true fundamental strength.

Economic indicators also provide insights into whether a market top is approaching. Rising interest rates are one of the strongest signals that a bull market may be ending. When central banks raise interest rates, borrowing becomes more expensive, reducing corporate profits and slowing economic growth. Historically, periods of aggressive rate hikes have preceded market declines, as higher interest rates reduce liquidity and lead to lower stock valuations. Similarly, rising inflation can erode purchasing power and force companies to increase prices, potentially leading to decreased consumer spending and weaker corporate earnings.

Another common characteristic of market tops is elevated levels of corporate buybacks and insider selling. When stock prices are elevated, companies often use excess cash to buy back shares, reducing the number of shares available and boosting earnings per share (EPS). While buybacks can be a sign of confidence, excessive buybacks at inflated valuations suggest that companies may be artificially inflating stock prices rather than reinvesting in growth. Likewise, insider selling—when company executives and board members sell substantial portions of their holdings—can indicate that those with the most knowledge of a company believe the stock is overvalued.

Investor sentiment indicators also help identify market tops. The Fear and Greed Index, which tracks investor emotions based on factors such as market momentum, volatility, and demand for safe-haven assets, often reaches extreme greed levels before a market correction. Elevated levels of margin debt—when investors borrow money to buy stocks—also signal overconfidence. When too many investors are using leverage to chase gains, the market becomes vulnerable to sharp declines if sentiment shifts.

While identifying market tops helps investors avoid losses, recognizing market bottoms allows for optimal buying opportunities. A market bottom occurs when stock prices reach their lowest point before rebounding, often following a prolonged period of pessimism, panic selling, and economic distress. These periods are marked by extreme fear, where investors abandon stocks due to uncertainty and negative headlines. However, history has shown that buying during times of fear, when valuations are at their lowest, leads to the highest long-term returns.

One of the best indicators of a market bottom is valuation compression. When P/E ratios fall significantly below historical averages and stocks trade at deep discounts compared to their intrinsic value, it often signals that the worst of the decline is over. During market bottoms, stocks of high-quality companies with strong fundamentals become undervalued simply because of broad market fear. Investors who recognize these mispricing's can take advantage of bargain prices before the next bull market begins.

Technical indicators also play a role in identifying market bottoms. Oversold conditions occur when stocks experience steep declines in a brief period, often reflected in technical indicators such as the Relative Strength Index (RSI) dropping below 30. This suggests that stocks may be due for a rebound. Additionally, moving average crossovers, such as the 200-day moving average flattening or turning upward after a prolonged downtrend, often indicate that selling pressure is easing and buyers are returning.

Another strong sign of a market bottom is capitulation, where investors panic and sell stocks indiscriminately. Capitulation events often involve high trading volumes, extreme volatility, and sharp price declines, followed by a stabilization period. These selloffs create conditions for market recoveries, as strong hands begin accumulating stocks at deeply discounted prices.

Economic indicators can also signal a market bottom. When central banks shift from raising interest rates to lowering them, liquidity increases, and stock prices often begin to recover. Additionally, if unemployment levels peak and economic data starts to improve, it suggests that the economy is stabilizing, which can fuel a stock market rebound. Historically, markets tend to recover before the economy fully rebounds, as investors anticipate better conditions ahead.

One of the biggest mistakes investors make is trying to time the exact top or bottom of the market. While recognizing these turning points is valuable, attempting to perfectly predict them is impossible. Instead, investors should focus on probability-based decision-making. If a market appears highly overvalued and speculative, reducing exposure or shifting into defensive assets can help protect capital.

Conversely, when a market appears deeply undervalued and fear dominates, gradually increasing exposure to high-quality stocks can lead to long-term gains.

A proven strategy for navigating market tops and bottoms is dollar-cost averaging (DCA), where investors buy stocks in small increments over time rather than trying to time the perfect entry. This approach reduces the risk of investing at extreme highs while ensuring exposure to undervalued opportunities during market declines. Investors who adopt a long-term perspective and focus on fundamentals rather than short-term price movements are better positioned to benefit from market cycles.

Recognizing market tops and bottoms requires a combination of fundamental analysis, technical indicators, economic data, and investor sentiment metrics. By staying informed and developing a disciplined investment approach, investors can avoid the pitfalls of speculative excess at market peaks while taking advantage of undervaluation at market lows. The key to long-term success is not perfect timing but smart decision-making based on evidence and probability. Markets move in cycles, and those who understand these cycles can navigate them effectively, maximizing gains while minimizing unnecessary risks.

4.3 How to Use Economic Indicators to Predict Market Trends and Improve Investment Timing

Investing successfully requires more than just analysing individual stocks; it also involves understanding the broader economic environment. Economic indicators provide valuable insights into market conditions, helping investors identify trends, anticipate changes in market sentiment, and make informed decisions about when to buy or sell stocks. While no single indicator can predict market movements with absolute certainty, a combination of key economic data points can offer a clearer picture of where the economy—and stock prices—are heading.

One of the most influential economic indicators is Gross Domestic Product (GDP), which measures the total value of goods and services produced within a country. GDP growth reflects the overall health of an economy—when GDP is expanding, businesses generate higher revenues, employment rises, and consumer spending increases, all of which support stock market growth. Conversely, when GDP growth slows or contracts, it can signal economic trouble, leading to market declines.

Investors should monitor GDP trends to assess whether the economy is in an expansion phase (bullish for stocks) or a recessionary phase (bearish for stocks). However, since GDP reports are released quarterly and reflect past data, they are often considered a lagging indicator—meaning they confirm economic trends rather than predict them.

A more forward-looking indicator is the Purchasing Managers' Index (PMI), which measures manufacturing and service sector activity. The PMI is considered one of the best real-time indicators of economic momentum because it reflects business confidence, new orders, production levels, and employment trends. A PMI reading above 50 indicates expansion, while a reading below 50 suggests contraction. When the PMI shows consistent declines, it can be an early warning sign that economic growth is slowing, which may lead to weaker corporate earnings and stock market corrections. Conversely, a rising PMI often signals a strengthening economy, supporting higher stock valuations.

Another critical economic indicator is unemployment data, particularly the Non-Farm Payroll (NFP) report and the unemployment rate. Strong job growth and low unemployment indicate a healthy economy, boosting consumer spending and corporate profits. However, if unemployment rises sharply, it often suggests that businesses are cutting costs due to declining demand, which can lead to weaker earnings, lower stock prices, and potential recessions. The challenge for investors is that stock markets often react to changes in unemployment expectations rather than the actual numbers. For example, if unemployment is low but starts trending upward, it could signal the beginning of an economic slowdown, prompting a market selloff even before GDP growth declines.

Interest rates, controlled by central banks such as the Federal Reserve (Fed), play a key role in stock market movements. When the Fed raises interest rates, borrowing costs for businesses and consumers increase, which can slow economic growth and put downward pressure on stock prices. High interest rates also make bonds and savings accounts more attractive, reducing investor demand for stocks. Conversely, when the Fed cuts interest rates, it stimulates borrowing, investment, and spending, often leading to stock market rallies. Investors should closely follow the Federal

Open Market Committee (FOMC) meetings, where policymakers discuss interest rate decisions and economic outlooks. The yield curve, which compares short-term and long-term interest rates, is also a key indicator—an inverted yield curve (when short-term rates are higher than long-term rates) has historically been a strong predictor of recessions.

Inflation is another major factor influencing stock market trends. Moderate inflation (around 2% annually) is healthy, as it reflects a growing economy. However, when inflation rises too quickly, it erodes consumer purchasing power and increases costs for businesses, leading to lower corporate profits. High inflation often prompts central banks to raise interest rates, which can negatively impact stock prices. Key inflation measures include the Consumer Price Index (CPI) and the Producer Price Index (PPI). When inflation data exceeds expectations, it can trigger market selloffs, especially in high-growth stocks that are more sensitive to interest rate hikes. On the other hand, declining inflation often signals improving economic conditions, supporting stock market gains.

Consumer spending is another crucial driver of stock market performance, as it accounts for a sizeable portion of GDP. Indicators such as Retail Sales Reports and the Consumer Confidence Index (CCI) provide insights into whether consumers are willing to spend or are cutting back due to economic uncertainty. Rising consumer confidence and strong retail sales numbers typically lead to higher corporate earnings, driving stock prices higher. Conversely, declining consumer sentiment can indicate future economic weakness, which may lead to stock market declines.

Corporate earnings report also serve as an important economic indicator. Publicly traded companies release quarterly earnings statements that provide insights into their revenue growth, profitability, and outlook. Earnings season, which occurs four times a year, often triggers market volatility as investors react to better-than-expected or worse-than-expected results. Monitoring earnings trends across different sectors helps investors understand which industries are thriving and which are struggling. For example, if technology companies consistently report strong earnings while retail companies report weak numbers, it may indicate shifts in consumer behaviour or economic conditions.

The stock market itself can serve as an early economic indicator, as it tends to move in anticipation of future economic conditions rather than react to past data. Historically, stock markets decline before recessions begin and start recovering before economic data improves. This is because investors price stocks based on expectations of future earnings, interest rates, and business conditions. Tracking market breadth indicators, such as the Advance-Decline Line (ADL) and moving averages, can provide insights into whether a market rally is broad-based and sustainable or driven by a handful of large stocks.

Another critical economic measure is commodity prices, particularly oil, gold, and industrial metals. Rising oil prices can indicate strong global demand but also contribute to inflation, which may lead to higher interest rates. Meanwhile, gold prices often rise during periods of economic uncertainty, as investors seek safe-haven assets. Industrial metals such as copper are closely tied to manufacturing activity—when copper prices rise, it often signals strong economic growth, while falling prices can indicate slowing industrial demand.

Geopolitical events and government policies also play a significant role in shaping market trends. Trade policies, regulatory changes, and fiscal stimulus programs can create both risks and opportunities for investors. For example, tax cuts and government spending programs often boost corporate profits and stock prices, while trade wars and regulatory crackdowns can create market uncertainty and volatility. Investors should pay attention to global economic events, as developments in major economies such as the U.S., China, and the European Union can have widespread effects on global markets.

Understanding how to interpret and use economic indicators allows investors to position their portfolios strategically. During periods of economic expansion, investors may favour growth stocks and cyclical sectors such as technology, consumer discretionary, and industrials. During economic slowdowns or recessions, defensive stocks—such as healthcare, utilities, and consumer staples—tend to outperform, as their earnings remain stable even in downturns. Interest rate-sensitive sectors, such as real estate and financials, also react strongly to central bank policies, providing additional opportunities for investors to adjust their holdings based on economic conditions.

While no single economic indicator guarantees market movements, combining multiple data points helps investors identify trends and make more informed decisions. Long-term success in investing requires not only selecting the right stocks but also understanding the broader economic forces that drive market cycles. By paying attention to GDP growth, interest rates, inflation, employment data, and market sentiment, investors can improve their ability to anticipate opportunities and avoid unnecessary risks, leading to better investment outcomes.

CHAPTER 5 – HOW TO BUILD A PROFITABLE STOCK PORTFOLIO

Building a profitable stock portfolio is more than just picking individual stocks. A successful investment strategy requires diversification, risk management, sector allocation, and a clear long-term plan. Many investors make the mistake of randomly selecting stocks without considering how they fit together within a broader strategy. Without a structured approach, portfolios can become unbalanced, exposing investors to excessive risk or limiting growth potential. A well-constructed portfolio ensures that investments are aligned with financial goals, risk tolerance, and market conditions, allowing for steady and sustainable wealth accumulation.

The first step in building a strong portfolio is defining investment objectives. Every investor has different financial goals, whether it is long-term wealth creation, passive income through dividends, retirement savings, or aggressive capital growth. Establishing clear objectives helps determine the right investment strategy, asset allocation, and risk tolerance. Investors seeking stable, long-term growth may focus on blue-chip stocks and diversified ETFs, while those looking for higher returns may allocate more capital to growth stocks, emerging markets, or technology companies. Understanding one's own risk tolerance is essential—some investors can manage market fluctuations, while others may prefer lower-volatility investments that offer steady but modest returns.

Once objectives are set, the next critical step is diversification. A portfolio should not rely too heavily on a single stock, sector, or industry. Diversification reduces risk by ensuring that losses in one area do not wipe out overall returns. A well-diversified portfolio includes stocks from different sectors, industries, and geographic regions. For example, technology stocks may offer high growth but can be volatile, while consumer staples and healthcare stocks tend to be more stable during market downturns. Investors should also diversify across market capitalizations—large-cap stocks provide stability, mid-cap stocks offer growth potential, and small-cap stocks can generate significant returns but come with higher risk. Geographic diversification further protects portfolios from country-specific economic risks. Investing in international markets, such as the U.S., Europe, and emerging economies, allows investors to benefit from global economic trends and reduce exposure to a single country's financial conditions.

Sector allocation is another crucial component of a profitable portfolio. While some investors try to "time" the market by rotating sectors based on economic cycles, a balanced allocation ensures steady performance across different market conditions. Key sectors include technology, healthcare, financials, consumer discretionary, industrials, energy, utilities, real estate, and materials. Each sector responds differently to market conditions—technology and consumer discretionary stocks thrive in economic booms, while utilities and healthcare stocks tend to perform well during downturns. Having exposure to multiple sectors allows investors to capture opportunities in various market environments while mitigating downside risks.

Dividend stocks can play a significant role in a well-structured portfolio, particularly for investors seeking passive income and financial stability. Companies that pay consistent dividends tend to be well-established, profitable, and financially resilient. Dividend-paying stocks also provide a buffer during market downturns, as investors continue to receive cash payments regardless of short-term price fluctuations. Investing in companies with a strong dividend history, consistent earnings growth, and a sustainable payout ratio ensures steady returns over time. Additionally, reinvesting dividends through dividend reinvestment plans (DRIPs) accelerates portfolio growth through compound interest, maximizing long-term returns.

Growth stocks are essential for investors aiming to outperform the market. Companies with high revenue growth, innovative products, and expanding market share often generate higher-than-average returns. However, growth stocks come with higher volatility, as they are more sensitive to economic cycles and investor sentiment. Balancing high-growth companies with stable dividend-paying stocks or defensive assets helps create a well-rounded portfolio. Evaluating key growth metrics such as revenue expansion, earnings per share (EPS) growth, profit margins, and return on equity (ROE) helps identify robust growth stocks with sustainable competitive advantages.

Another critical aspect of portfolio construction is risk management. While higher returns often come with increased risk, a well-balanced portfolio minimizes unnecessary exposure to extreme volatility. Setting appropriate position sizes for each stock prevents overexposure to a single company or sector. Many professional investors limit individual stock positions to 5% or less of their total portfolio to avoid excessive risk. Additionally, setting stop-loss levels—automatic triggers that sell stocks when they decline beyond a certain percentage—helps protect against severe downturns. Stop-loss orders ensure that investors exit bad investments before significant losses accumulate, allowing capital to be reallocated into stronger opportunities.

Investors should also be mindful of market cycles when building their portfolios. Economic conditions influence stock performance, and adjusting exposure based on macroeconomic trends can enhance returns. During bull markets, investors may increase exposure to growth and technology stocks, while in bear markets, shifting capital toward defensive sectors like healthcare, utilities, and consumer staples helps preserve wealth. Holding cash or fixed-income assets during periods of extreme market uncertainty provides liquidity and the flexibility to buy undervalued stocks when opportunities arise.

Portfolio rebalancing is a key strategy for maintaining a profitable portfolio over time. As stock prices fluctuate, portfolio weightings shift, potentially increasing risk exposure or altering investment objectives. Periodic rebalancing—typically every six months or annually—ensures that investments remain aligned with financial goals. If one sector or stock significantly outperforms, investors may need to trim profits and reallocate funds into undervalued areas to maintain diversification. This disciplined approach prevents emotional decision-making and enhances long-term returns.

One of the biggest mistakes investors make is failing to adapt their portfolios to changing market conditions, new opportunities, and personal financial goals. Regularly reviewing holdings, evaluating company performance, and staying informed about economic trends allows investors to make data-driven decisions rather than reacting emotionally to short-term fluctuations. While a buy-and-hold strategy works well for long-term investors, occasional adjustments based on market conditions, industry shifts, and financial objectives can optimize portfolio performance.

Using exchange-traded funds (ETFs) and mutual funds can further strengthen a stock portfolio by providing broad market exposure with lower risk. ETFs track specific indices, sectors, or asset classes, allowing investors to gain diversification without needing to select individual stocks. Low-cost ETFs focused on the S&P 500, dividend-paying stocks, emerging markets, or specific sectors can complement an actively managed stock portfolio, reducing overall volatility while capturing market growth.

Tax efficiency is another crucial factor when managing a profitable stock portfolio. Holding investments in tax-advantaged accounts such as IRAs or 401(k)s can minimize tax liabilities, allowing investments to compound over time without unnecessary tax burdens. Investors should also consider tax-loss harvesting, a strategy where losing investments are sold to offset capital gains taxes, reducing overall tax exposure. Understanding tax implications ensures that profits are maximized while minimizing unnecessary tax costs.

A long-term mindset is essential for building a profitable stock portfolio. The stock market experiences short-term fluctuations, but history has shown that investors who remain patient and disciplined generate superior returns over decades. Avoiding frequent trading, resisting emotional reactions to market movements, and staying focused on fundamentals rather than speculation are hallmarks of successful investors. Legendary investors like Warren Buffett emphasize buying high-quality companies and holding them for the long term, allowing compounding returns to work in their Favor.

Building a profitable stock portfolio requires careful planning, diversification, risk management, and a strong understanding of economic trends. A well-structured portfolio includes a mix of growth stocks, dividend stocks, sector diversification, and risk-control strategies. Investors who develop a clear investment strategy, regularly review their holdings, and stay informed about market conditions position themselves for long-term success. The key to wealth-building in the stock market is not chasing quick profits but consistently investing in strong companies, managing risk wisely, and allowing time to work in your Favor.

5.1 How to Allocate Your Portfolio for Maximum Returns and Minimum Risk

One of the most critical aspects of building a successful stock portfolio is proper allocation—the way investments are distributed across different asset classes, sectors, and individual stocks. Portfolio allocation plays a key role in balancing risk and reward, ensuring that investments are aligned with financial goals, risk tolerance, and market conditions. Many investors make the mistake of concentrating too much in one area, which can lead to high volatility and increased exposure to market downturns. A well-allocated portfolio, on the other hand, provides stability, consistent returns, and resilience across different market conditions.

The first step in portfolio allocation is determining the right mix of asset classes. Stocks are an essential component of any growth-oriented portfolio, but a well-diversified investment strategy may also include bonds, real estate, commodities, and cash equivalents. Each asset class serves a different purpose—stocks drive long-term growth, bonds provide stability and income, real estate offers inflation protection, and cash ensures liquidity during market downturns. The percentage allocated to each asset class depends on an investor's risk tolerance, time horizon, and financial goals.

Age-based allocation models provide a starting point for balancing risk and reward. Younger investors with a long-time horizon can afford to take more risk, allocating a higher percentage of their portfolio to stocks (typically 80-90%) while keeping a smaller portion in bonds and cash. As investors approach retirement, a more conservative allocation is recommended to preserve wealth, with a shift toward income-generating investments like bonds, dividend stocks, and real estate. A common rule of thumb is "100 minus your age" to determine the percentage of a portfolio that should be in stocks—for example, a 30-year-old might allocate 70-80% to stocks, while a 60-year-old may reduce stock exposure to 40-50%.

Within the stock portion of a portfolio, proper sector diversification is crucial for reducing risk and capitalizing on different economic cycles. The stock market is divided into several key sectors, including technology, healthcare, consumer discretionary, consumer staples, financials, industrials, energy, utilities, real estate, and materials. Each sector performs differently based on economic conditions, interest rates, and consumer demand. For example, technology and consumer discretionary stocks tend to outperform during economic expansions, while healthcare, utilities, and consumer staples provide stability during recessions. Allocating investments across multiple sectors ensures that portfolio performance is not entirely dependent on the success of a single industry.

Market capitalization is another crucial factor in portfolio allocation. Investors should diversify among large-cap, mid-cap, and small-cap stocks, as each category offers different risk-reward profiles. Large-cap stocks (companies with market values over $10 billion) tend to be stable and well-established, making them ideal for long-term, low-risk investments. Mid-cap stocks ($2-$10 billion) offer a balance between stability and growth potential, often outperforming large-cap stocks while still maintaining lower risk than small-cap stocks. Small-cap stocks (under $2 billion) have the highest growth potential but also come with greater volatility and risk. A balanced portfolio may include 60% large-cap stocks, 25% mid-cap stocks, and 15% small-cap stocks, depending on risk tolerance.

Geographic diversification also enhances portfolio resilience by reducing dependence on a single country's economy. While U.S. stocks dominate global markets, adding international exposure through European, Asian, and emerging market stocks provides access to global growth opportunities. Emerging markets, such as China, India, and Brazil, offer higher growth potential but come with greater political and economic risk, while developed markets like Europe and Japan provide stability and steady returns. Investing in international ETFs or global mutual funds makes it easier to gain diversified exposure to different regions without having to pick individual stocks.

A well-allocated portfolio should also include a mix of growth stocks and dividend stocks. Growth stocks—companies that reinvest earnings to expand rapidly—

typically deliver higher capital appreciation but come with greater volatility. These stocks include companies in the technology, e-commerce, and biotechnology industries. Dividend stocks, on the other hand, offer consistent income and stability, making them valuable for long-term investors. Companies with a strong history of dividend payments tend to be financially healthy, providing returns even during market downturns. Allocating 50-70% to growth stocks and 30-50% to dividend stocks balances capital appreciation with income generation.

Another key principle in portfolio allocation is risk-adjusted investing, which ensures that each investment contributes to overall portfolio stability rather than increasing unnecessary risk. One way to manage risk is by setting position size limits—for example, limiting any single stock to no more than 5-10% of the total portfolio. This prevents overexposure to any one company and minimizes the impact of individual stock fluctuations. Investors can also implement stop-loss strategies, which automatically sell a stock if it declines beyond a certain percentage, protecting against major losses.

Liquidity is another crucial factor to consider in portfolio allocation. While long-term investors should focus on holding quality stocks for years, having liquid assets available for emergencies or market opportunities is essential. Keeping 5-10% of a portfolio in cash or short-term bonds allows investors to take advantage of stock market downturns and buy undervalued companies at attractive prices. During bear markets, having cash reserves ensures that investors can continue investing without being forced to sell assets at a loss.

Rebalancing a portfolio regularly is crucial for maintaining the desired allocation over time. As stock prices fluctuate, certain sectors or asset classes may become overweight or underweight, shifting the portfolio's risk profile. Reviewing investments every six months or annually and reallocating funds into underperforming areas helps maintain diversification and prevents excessive exposure to high-risk assets. Rebalancing also provides an opportunity to take profits from overperforming stocks and reinvest in undervalued opportunities.

Investors should also consider the role of ETFs and index funds in portfolio allocation. Exchange-traded funds (ETFs) offer broad market exposure with lower fees, making them an excellent option for passive investors. ETFs that track the S&P 500, Nasdaq, dividend stocks, emerging markets, or specific industries provide diversification while minimizing individual stock risk. Combining ETFs with individual stocks allows investors to capture market-wide growth while maintaining control over stock selection.

Risk tolerance plays a significant role in portfolio allocation. Some investors are comfortable with high-risk, high-reward portfolios, while others prefer low-volatility investments that provide steady, predictable returns. Investors should assess their risk tolerance regularly and adjust their allocation accordingly. Factors such as income stability, time horizon, and investment experience all influence the appropriate level of risk exposure. For those seeking a conservative approach, allocating more capital to dividend-paying stocks, bonds, and defensive sectors ensures lower volatility. For aggressive investors, focusing on high-growth industries, innovation-driven companies, and emerging markets can maximize long-term returns.

Tax efficiency is another key consideration in portfolio allocation. Holding investments in tax-advantaged accounts such as IRAs, 401(k)s, and Roth IRAs reduces the impact of capital gains taxes and dividend taxes. Investors should also implement tax-loss harvesting strategies, which involve selling losing investments to offset taxable gains, lowering overall tax liabilities. Choosing tax-efficient investment vehicles, such as index funds with low turnover, minimizes taxable distributions and improves after-tax returns.

The best investment portfolios are built with long-term vision and disciplined execution. Rather than chasing short-term gains or reacting emotionally to market movements, investors should focus on consistently applying a structured allocation strategy that balances risk, reward, and financial goals. Staying diversified, adjusting allocations based on market conditions, and periodically reviewing holdings ensures that the portfolio remains aligned with long-term objectives. Successful investors understand that portfolio allocation is not about chasing the hottest stocks but about creating a resilient strategy that generates steady and reliable growth over time.

5.2 How to Evaluate Stocks Before Adding Them to Your Portfolio

Building a strong and profitable stock portfolio requires careful evaluation of each stock before making an investment decision. Many investors make the mistake of buying stocks based on hype, recommendations, or recent price movements without conducting proper due diligence. However, long-term success in the stock market comes from investing in companies with strong fundamentals, reasonable valuations, and solid growth potential. This chapter provides a structured approach to evaluating stocks before adding them to a portfolio, ensuring that every investment decision is based on data, logic, and financial health rather than speculation.

Step 1: Understanding the Business Model and Competitive Advantage

Before investing in any stock, it is crucial to understand what the company does, how it makes money, and whether it has a competitive advantage. Many successful investors, including Warren Buffett, emphasize the importance of investing in companies with a strong economic moat—a sustainable advantage that protects the company from competitors.

A strong economic moat can come from various sources:

- **Brand Power:** Companies like Apple, Coca-Cola, and Nike have powerful brands that create customer loyalty, allowing them to charge premium prices.
- **Network Effects:** Businesses like Meta (Facebook) and Visa benefit from a growing number of users, making their services more valuable over time.
- **Cost Advantages:** Amazon and Walmart use economies of scale to offer lower prices than competitors, making it difficult for new entrants to compete.
- **Patents and Intellectual Property:** Pharmaceutical companies like Pfizer and biotech firms protect their innovations with patents, giving them exclusive rights to sell certain products.

To assess a company's competitive advantage, ask the following questions:

- What makes this company unique compared to competitors?
- Can new competitors easily enter this industry and take market share?
- Does the company have pricing power, allowing it to raise prices without losing customers?

- Has the company maintained a strong position in its industry over the past five to ten years?

Step 2: Analysing Financial Health and Stability

A company with a strong business model is not always a worthwhile investment—financial stability is equally important. Before buying a stock, investors should analyse key financial statements, including the income statement, balance sheet, and cash flow statement.

Key Financial Metrics to Evaluate:

- **Revenue Growth** – Is the company consistently increasing its revenue? Look at the past five years of revenue growth to determine if the business is expanding.
- **Earnings Per Share (EPS) Growth** – A company that grows earnings consistently is likely to create value for shareholders. Rising EPS over time is a positive sign.
- **Profit Margins** – Companies with high profit margins are more efficient and resilient. Compare gross margin, operating margin, and net margin to industry peers.
- **Return on Equity (ROE) and Return on Invested Capital (ROIC)** – These metrics measure how efficiently a company generates profits from its capital. A high ROE (above 15%) and ROIC (above 10%) indicate strong financial performance.
- **Debt Levels (Debt-to-Equity Ratio)** – Too much debt can be risky. A debt-to-equity ratio below 1.0 is considered safe, though this varies by industry.
- **Free Cash Flow (FCF)** – This shows how much cash a company generates after expenses. Consistently positive FCF indicates a company has enough cash to reinvest, pay dividends, or reduce debt.

Example of Financial Analysis:

Imagine you are evaluating two companies in the same industry:

Metric	Company A	Company B
Revenue Growth (5 years)	+12%	+3%
EPS Growth (5 years)	+15%	-2%
Gross Margin	48%	32%
Debt-to-Equity Ratio	0.5	2.1
Free Cash Flow	Positive	Negative

Company A has strong revenue and earnings growth, higher margins, lower debt, and positive free cash flow, making it a better investment candidate than Company B.

Step 3: Evaluating Stock Valuation

Even if a company has strong financials, it must be priced before making an investment. Investors use valuation metrics to determine whether a stock is overvalued, undervalued, or fairly priced.

Key Valuation Metrics:

- **Price-to-Earnings (P/E) Ratio** – Compares a stock's price to its earnings. A lower P/E relative to industry peers may indicate undervaluation.
- **Price-to-Book (P/B) Ratio** – Measures stock price relative to book value. A P/B below 1.5 suggests the stock may be undervalued.
- **Price-to-Sales (P/S) Ratio** – Compares stock price to revenue. A P/S below 2.0 is usually considered an excellent value.
- **PEG Ratio (P/E to Growth Rate)** – A PEG below 1.0 indicates the stock is undervalued relative to its growth rate.
- **Dividend Yield (if applicable)** – If the company pays dividends, check the dividend yield and payout ratio to ensure the dividend is sustainable.

Example of Valuation Analysis:

Metric	Company A	Company B	Industry Average
P/E Ratio	18	30	22
P/B Ratio	2.0	4.5	3.0
P/S Ratio	1.8	3.2	2.5
PEG Ratio	0.9	2.1	1.5

Company A has a lower P/E, P/B, and P/S ratio compared to Company B and the industry average. It also has a PEG ratio below 1.0, suggesting it is undervalued relative to its growth potential.

Step 4: Assessing Market Trends and Timing the Purchase

Even if a stock is financially strong and valued, market conditions can impact investment success. Understanding industry trends, macroeconomic factors, and technical indicators can help determine the best time to buy.

- **Is the stock in an uptrend or downtrend?** Buying stocks in an uptrend can improve short-term returns.
- **Are interest rates rising or falling**? Rising interest rates can hurt growth stocks, while lower rates benefit them.
- **Are there upcoming earnings reports?** Buying before earnings can be risky if the stock experiences volatility.
- Using technical indicators like moving averages, support levels, and RSI (Relative Strength Index) can refine entry points.

Exercise: Stock Evaluation Checklist

To practice evaluating stocks, complete the following checklist for a company of your choice:

What is the company's business model and competitive advantage?

Does the company have stable revenue and earnings growth?

Are profit margins and free cash flow strong?

Is the company's debt manageable?

What is the stock's valuation compared to industry peers?

Are there any external risks affecting the company or industry?

Is the stock in an uptrend or near a dedicated support level?

By following this step-by-step evaluation process, investors can make informed decisions, reduce risk, and build a high-quality stock portfolio that delivers consistent long-term returns. Conducting thorough research before buying a stock ensures that every investment is strategic, data-driven, and aligned with financial goals.

5.3 How to Manage and Monitor Your Portfolio for Long-Term Success

Building a stock portfolio is only the first step toward successful investing. Ongoing management and monitoring are essential to ensure that investments continue to align with financial goals, risk tolerance, and changing market conditions. Many investors make the mistake of buying stocks and forgetting about them, assuming they will automatically grow over time. However, even the strongest companies can face challenges, and market conditions can shift. Regularly reviewing and adjusting a portfolio helps maximize returns, manage risk, and maintain a balanced allocation.

Step 1: Setting Up a Portfolio Monitoring System

To effectively track investments, investors should establish a structured monitoring process that includes key performance indicators, alerts for significant price movements, and periodic reviews. A well-organized system prevents emotional decision-making and ensures that investment decisions are based on data rather than market noise.

Tools for Portfolio Tracking:

- **Brokerage Account Dashboards** – Most online brokers provide tools for tracking performance, dividends, and asset allocation.
- **Spreadsheets** – Custom Excel or Google Sheets can track stock prices, purchase dates, total returns, and diversification levels.
- **Stock Market Apps** – Apps like Yahoo Finance, Morningstar, and Seeking Alpha provide real-time data, earnings reports, and news updates.
- **Automated Alerts** – Setting alerts for stock price movements, earnings releases, and major news events ensures timely reactions.

Investors should track the following key metrics for each stock in their portfolio:

- **Current Price vs. Purchase Price** – Is the stock performing as expected?
- **Earnings Growth** – Are earnings increasing in line with company projections?
- **Dividend Payments (if applicable)** – Is the company maintaining or increasing dividends?
- **Valuation Metrics (P/E, P/B, PEG, etc.)** – Has the stock become overvalued or undervalued?
- **Market Trends and Economic Conditions** – Are broader market trends affecting the stock's performance?

Step 2: Setting Review Intervals for Portfolio Adjustments

Successful investors regularly review their portfolios to ensure that each stock remains a strong investment. However, checking stock prices daily can lead to emotional trading decisions, which often hurt long-term returns. Instead, a structured quarterly or semi-annual review process is recommended.

Recommended Portfolio Review Frequency:

- **Monthly CheckIn** – Quick performance check to ensure no drastic changes.
- **Quarterly Review** – Evaluate earnings reports, sector performance, and macroeconomic conditions.
- **Annual Review** – Rebalance allocations, reassess financial goals, and adjust holdings accordingly.

During each review, investors should answer these questions:

- **Has my original investment thesis changed?**
- **Are my stocks still fundamentally strong?**
- **Am I properly diversified, or do I need to adjust allocations?**
- **Do I need to sell any underperforming** stocks or take profits from overvalued positions?

Step 3: Knowing When to Sell a Stock

Selling stocks is just as important as buying them, yet many investors struggle with knowing when to exit an investment. Holding onto losing stocks for too long in hopes of a recovery or selling winning stocks too early due to fear of a decline are common mistakes.

Valid Reasons to Sell a Stock:

- **The Company's Fundamentals Have Weakened** – If revenue growth slows, profit margins shrink, or debt levels rise significantly, it may signal trouble.
- **The Stock Becomes Overvalued** – If valuation metrics (P/E, PEG, P/B) are far above industry averages, it may be time to take profits.
- **Better Investment Opportunities Exist** – If another stock offers better growth potential or a more attractive risk-reward ratio, reallocating capital can improve portfolio performance.
- **Market Conditions Have Changed** – Economic downturns, rising interest rates, or sector-specific challenges may impact stock performance.

- **Portfolio Rebalancing Is Needed** – If a single stock or sector has grown too large within the portfolio, trimming the position reduces concentration risk.

Example of a Sell Decision:

Imagine an investor holds Company X, which was purchased at $50 per share with a P/E ratio of 15. Over the next three years, the stock price rises to $150 per share, and the P/E ratio expands to 40. Meanwhile, revenue growth slows, and competitors gain market share. In this case, selling at a high valuation while fundamentals weaken could prevent losses from a future downturn.

Step 4: Portfolio Rebalancing to Maintain Proper Allocation

Over time, certain stocks or sectors may outperform others, leading to imbalanced asset allocation. Rebalancing ensures that a portfolio remains aligned with an investor's original strategy and risk tolerance.

Rebalancing Strategies:

- **Trim Overperforming Stocks** – If one stock grows to represent more than 10% of the portfolio, selling a portion lock in gains and reduces risk.
- **Increase Exposure to Undervalued Stocks** – Buying stocks that are temporarily out of favour but still fundamentally strong can enhance returns.
- **Adjust Sector Exposure** – Shifting allocations based on economic cycles ensures resilience in different market environments.

For example, if an investor originally allocated 60% to stocks, 30% to bonds, and 10% to cash, but due to a bull market stocks now make up 75% of the portfolio, rebalancing would involve selling some stocks and reallocating funds into bonds or cash to restore balance.

Step 5: Managing Risk with Stop-Loss and Exit Strategies

Risk management is essential for preserving capital and avoiding catastrophic losses. Setting stop-loss levels—where stocks are automatically sold if they decline beyond a predetermined percentage—protects against unexpected downturns.

Types of Stop-Loss Strategies:

- **Fixed Percentage Stop-Loss** – Selling a stock if it drops by 15-20% from the purchase price.
- **Trailing Stop-Loss** – Adjusting the stop-loss as the stock price increases to lock in gains while protecting downside risk.
- **Fundamental Stop-Loss** – Selling if earnings decline, profit margins shrink, or the company loses competitive strength.

For example, if an investor buys a stock at $100 and sets a 20% stop-loss, the stock will be sold if it drops to $80, preventing further losses. If the stock rises to $150, a trailing stop-loss at 10% ensures it is sold if it declines to $135, locking in profits.

Step 6: Adapting to Market Conditions and Economic Trends

Stock market conditions constantly change, and investors who adapt their strategies accordingly can improve portfolio performance.

How to Adjust Based on Market Conditions:

- **During Bull Markets** – Increase exposure to growth stocks and cyclical sectors (technology, consumer discretionary, industrials).
- **During Bear Markets** – Shift towards defensive sectors and dividend stocks (healthcare, utilities, consumer staples).
- **During High Inflation Periods** – Invest in commodity stocks, real estate, and energy sectors that benefit from rising prices.
- **During Low-Interest Rate Environments** – Focus on growth stocks and high-dividend payers, as lower rates reduce borrowing costs.

For example, in 2022, rising inflation and interest rate hikes led to declines in high-growth technology stocks, while energy and commodity stocks outperformed. Investors who adjusted their portfolios accordingly benefited from these shifts.

Step 7: Avoiding Common Portfolio Management Mistakes

Even experienced investors can fall into behavioural traps that harm long-term returns. Avoiding these mistakes improves overall success.

Common Portfolio Management Mistakes to Avoid:

- **Overtrading** – Constantly buying and selling stocks increases transaction costs and taxes.

- **Chasing Hot Stocks** – Investing in stocks just because they are rising can lead to losses when momentum fades.
- **Ignoring Diversification** – Concentrating too much in one sector increases risk.
- **Holding on to Losing Stocks Too Long** – Selling underperformers and reallocating capital to better opportunities prevents further losses.

By following a structured portfolio management approach, investors can maximize returns, minimize risk, and maintain a well-balanced investment strategy that withstands market fluctuations. Long-term success in the stock market comes from disciplined decision-making, consistent portfolio reviews, and adapting to changing conditions while avoiding emotional reactions.

CHAPTER 6 – HOW TO MANAGE STOCK MARKET VOLATILITY LIKE A PROFESSIONAL INVESTOR

Stock market volatility is inevitable. Prices fluctuate daily due to economic data, corporate earnings, geopolitical events, and investor sentiment. While volatility can create stress and uncertainty, successful investors understand how to navigate market swings without letting emotions dictate their decisions. Instead of fearing volatility, professional investors use it to their advantage by identifying opportunities, managing risk, and staying disciplined in their investment strategies. Learning how to manage stock market volatility like a professional ensures long-term success while avoiding costly mistakes driven by fear or greed.

Understanding the Nature of Stock Market Volatility

Volatility refers to the degree of price movement in stocks or the market. Markets experience periods of stability, gradual increases, sharp drops, and recoveries. While short-term fluctuations may seem unpredictable, volatility follows certain patterns based on economic cycles, interest rates, corporate performance, and investor behaviour.

Historically, the stock market has experienced numerous corrections (declines of 10% or more) and bear markets (declines of 20% or more), yet it has always recovered and continued to grow over time. For example, the S&P 500 has averaged an annual return of about 10% over the past century, despite experiencing multiple recessions, financial crises, and geopolitical shocks. Understanding that volatility is normal helps investors remain patient and avoid panic-driven decisions.

The Emotional Challenges of Market Volatility

Emotions such as fear, and greed often cause investors to react irrationally during volatile periods. When stock prices fall, fear drives panic selling, leading investors to lock in losses instead of waiting for a recovery. Conversely, during bull markets, greed encourages investors to chase high-flying stocks, often leading to buying at inflated prices before a correction occurs.

Common emotional mistakes during volatility include:

- **Selling at the Bottom** – Many investors panic and sell stocks after a sharp decline, missing potential rebounds.
- **Chasing Momentum Stocks** – Buying stocks that have already surged often leads to losses when the trend reverses.
- **Ignoring Fundamentals** – Focusing on short-term price swings rather than company fundamentals leads to poor investment decisions.
- **Overtrading** – Frequent buying and selling in response to market swings results in higher transaction costs and reduced returns.

Proven Strategies to Manage Volatility Like a Professional

Professional investors manage market volatility by sticking to proven strategies that allow them to stay focused on long-term goals while taking advantage of market fluctuations.

1. Stay Focused on Long-Term Fundamentals

Stock prices fluctuate daily, but a company's long-term value is based on fundamentals, not short-term movements. Strong businesses with solid revenue growth, profitability, and competitive advantages tend to recover from downturns and continue growing over time. Instead of reacting to volatility, professional investors focus on whether a company's underlying fundamentals remain strong.

For example, during the 2020 market crash, many investors sold stocks due to panic, while professionals bought shares of companies like Apple, Amazon, and Microsoft, knowing their long-term growth potential remained intact. Those who stayed invested benefited from the subsequent market rebound.

2. Use Volatility as a Buying Opportunity

Market downturns often create discounted buying opportunities for high-quality stocks. When fear drives stock prices lower, professional investors look for undervalued companies with strong fundamentals. Instead of fearing volatility, they capitalize on lower prices by accumulating shares at a discount.

A useful strategy during downturns is dollar-cost averaging (DCA)—investing a fixed amount at regular intervals regardless of market conditions. This strategy reduces the impact of short-term fluctuations and ensures that investors buy more shares when prices are low.

Example: If an investor wants to invest $12,000 in a stock, instead of buying all at once, they can invest $1,000 per month for 12 months. If the stock price drops during that period, they automatically buy more shares at a lower price, improving long-term returns.

3. Maintain a Diversified Portfolio

Diversification spreads investments across different sectors, asset classes, and geographic regions, reducing the impact of volatility on a portfolio. Instead of relying on a few stocks or industries, professional investors balance their portfolios with a mix of growth stocks, defensive stocks, dividend-paying stocks, and alternative investments.

During bear markets, defensive sectors like healthcare, consumer staples, and utilities tend to perform better than cyclical industries like technology or consumer discretionary. Holding a mix of stocks, bonds, and commodities helps stabilize returns when equity markets are volatile.

Example of a diversified portfolio:

- 50% in growth stocks (technology, e-commerce, emerging industries)
- 25% in defensive stocks (healthcare, utilities, consumer staples)
- 15% in dividend stocks (stable companies with consistent cash flow)
- 10% in alternative assets (gold, real estate, or bonds for stability)

This structure allows investors to participate in market growth while having protection during downturns.

4. Avoid Market Timing – Stay Invested

Trying to predict when the market will crash, or recover is impossible. Many investors sell stocks expecting a correction, only to miss the best days of market rebounds. Professional investors stay invested through all market conditions, knowing that missing just a few strong rally days can significantly impact returns.

Historical data shows that missing the best-performing days in the market results in lower overall returns. Instead of trying to time the market, investors should focus on time in the market—holding strong investments for the long term.

Example: If an investor had stayed fully invested in the S&P 500 from 1990 to 2020, they would have earned an average annual return of around 10%. However, if they missed just the best 10 days, their returns would have dropped significantly.

5. Use Stop-Loss and Risk Management Strategies

While long-term investing is key, risk management protects capital during extreme volatility. Professional investors use stop-loss orders, trailing stops, and hedging strategies to limit downside risk.

- **Stop-Loss Orders** – Automatically sell a stock if it drops below a predetermined price, preventing further losses.
- **Trailing Stops** – Adjust stop-loss levels as a stock price rises, locking in gains while protecting against reversals.
- **Hedging with Options** – Advanced investors use put options or inverse ETFs to protect portfolios from large market declines.

For example, if an investor buys a stock at $100, they may set a stop-loss at $80 to limit downside risk. If the stock rises to $150, they can use a trailing stop at $135, ensuring they capture most of the gains even if the stock declines.

6. Control Emotions and Stick to the Investment Plan

Professional investors remove emotions from their investment process by following a structured plan. Setting clear buy and sell criteria, defining risk levels, and focusing on long-term objectives prevent impulsive decisions.

Successful investors follow predefined investment rules, such as:

- Only selling a stock if fundamentals deteriorate, not due to short-term price drops.
- Rebalancing a portfolio every 6-12 months instead of reacting to daily news.
- Sticking to a long-term investment horizon, regardless of short-term volatility.

- By following a disciplined approach, investors avoid emotional mistakes and improve long-term performance.

Market volatility is unavoidable, but it does not have to be a source of fear or stress. Investors who develop a calm, disciplined approach can use volatility to buy undervalued stocks, diversify portfolios, and manage risk effectively. By staying focused on fundamentals, avoiding emotional decisions, and maintaining a long-term perspective, investors can navigate any market condition with confidence. Instead of fearing volatility, embracing it as an opportunity allows investors to build wealth over time and achieve financial success in the stock market.

6.1 How to Identify and Take Advantage of Market Corrections

Market corrections—defined as a decline of 10% or more from recent highs—are a natural part of stock market cycles. While many investors panic during corrections, professional investors view them as opportunities to buy high-quality stocks at discounted prices. Understanding why corrections happen, how to recognize them early, and how to capitalize on them can turn short-term market declines into long-term gains.

What Causes Market Corrections?

Market corrections occur due to a variety of factors, including economic shifts, interest rate changes, geopolitical events, and investor sentiment. Some of the most common reasons corrections happen include:

- **Overvaluation of Stocks** – When stock prices rise too quickly without supporting earnings growth, the market often corrects to bring valuations back to reasonable levels.
- **Rising Interest Rates** – Higher interest rates make borrowing more expensive, slowing economic growth and causing investors to reassess stock valuations.
- Inflation Concerns – If inflation rises too fast, it can reduce corporate profits and trigger a selloff in stocks.
- **Geopolitical Events** – Wars, trade disputes, and political instability create uncertainty, leading investors to pull money out of riskier assets.

- **Earnings Disappointments** – When major companies report lower-than-expected earnings, it can lead to widespread selling across the market.
- **Market Sentiment Shifts** – Investor emotions drive short-term market movements. If optimism turns into fear, selling pressure can push stocks lower.

While these factors can cause short-term declines, market corrections are different from bear markets. A correction is a temporary adjustment that usually lasts a few weeks to a few months, while a bear market (a drop of 20% or more) often signals a prolonged economic slowdown.

How to Identify When a Market Correction is Happening

Recognizing a correction early allows investors to adjust their strategies accordingly. Some key signs that a correction is underway include:

- **Broad Market Declines** – Major indices like the S&P 500, Nasdaq, or Dow Jones Industrial Average drop by 10% or more from their recent highs.
- **Increased Volatility** – The CBOE Volatility Index (VIX), often called the "fear index," spikes higher, indicating uncertainty in the market.
- **High Trading Volume** – A surge in selling activity, especially in large-cap stocks, suggests that institutional investors are exiting positions.
- **Sector Weakness** – Cyclical sectors (like technology and consumer discretionary) decline faster than defensive sectors (like healthcare and utilities).
- **Investor Panic and Negative Headlines** – News outlets and analysts become increasingly pessimistic, often predicting further declines.

While it is impossible to predict exactly when a correction will start or end, these indicators help investors determine when the market is experiencing short-term turbulence.

What Investors Should Do During a Market Correction

Instead of panicking, successful investors use market corrections to strengthen their portfolios and buy high-quality stocks at lower prices. Here is how to take advantage of a correction:

1. Avoid Emotional Reactions and Stick to Your Investment Plan

One of the biggest mistakes investors make is selling stocks out of fear when prices drop. Selling during a correction lock in losses and prevents investors from benefiting from a future rebound. History shows that corrections are temporary, and markets typically recover within months.

Example:

In March 2020, the S&P 500 dropped 35% in just one month due to the COVID-19 pandemic. Many investors panicked and sold their stocks. However, within six months, the market had recovered fully, and those who stayed invested saw their portfolios grow significantly.

To prevent emotional selling, investors should focus on the long-term fundamentals of their holdings rather than short-term price movements.

2. Identify High-Quality Stocks That Are Undervalued

Market corrections often drag strong companies down along with weaker ones. This presents a rare opportunity to buy shares of industry leaders at lower prices. Investors should look for stocks that have:

- Consistent revenue and earnings growth
- High return on equity (ROE) and return on invested capital (ROIC)
- Low debt levels and strong balance sheets
- A sustainable competitive advantage (economic moat)

A stock that was previously too expensive may become a great buying opportunity after a 10-15% decline.

Example:

Suppose Apple (AAPL) was trading at a P/E ratio of 30 before a correction. After a market-wide selloff, the stock drops 15%, bringing the P/E ratio down to 22—closer to its historical average. This could indicate that the stock is now valued or undervalued, making it a buying opportunity.

3. Use Dollar-Cost Averaging (DCA) to Buy Stocks Gradually

Instead of trying to time the exact bottom of a correction, investors can use dollar-cost averaging (DCA) to buy stocks in small increments over time. This strategy reduces risk by spreading out purchases and ensuring that investors buy at different price levels.

Example:

If an investor wants to invest $10,000 in a stock during a correction, they can divide the amount into four purchases of $2,500 over a few weeks. If the stock price continues to drop, they buy more shares at a lower price, improving their average cost.

4. Rebalance Your Portfolio

Market corrections can shift portfolio allocations, causing certain sectors or stocks to become overweight or underweight. Investors should use corrections to rebalance their portfolios by:

- Trimming overperforming stocks and reallocating capital into undervalued stocks.
- Increasing exposure to defensive sectors like consumer staples, utilities, and healthcare.
- Reducing high-risk speculative positions that may struggle in a downturn.
- Portfolio rebalancing ensures that risk remains controlled while maintaining diversification.

5. Keep Cash Reserves for Future Opportunities

While staying invested is important, having cash available during corrections allows investors to buy stocks at lower prices without selling existing holdings. Professional investors always keep a portion of their portfolio in cash or short-term bonds to take advantage of market pullbacks.

Example:

If an investor keeps 10-15% of their portfolio in cash, they can deploy this capital when stocks experience a 10-20% decline, capturing bargain prices.

6. Monitor Economic Indicators to Predict When the Market Will Recover

While it is impossible to time the exact bottom, certain economic indicators can signal when a market correction is nearing its end:

- **Improving corporate earnings** – If companies begin reporting better-than-expected earnings, it suggests business conditions are stabilizing.
- **Federal Reserve policy changes** – If interest rates are lowered, it can provide a boost to stock prices.
- **Rising consumer confidence** – If consumer spending starts increasing again, it indicates economic recovery.
- **Stock market technical indicators** – When major indices break above their 50-day or 200-day moving averages, it often signals the end of a correction.

Investors who wait for these signals before making large investments can increase their chances of buying near the bottom of a correction.

Turning Market Corrections into Opportunities

Instead of fearing market corrections, smart investors use them to strengthen their portfolios, buy quality stocks at discounted prices, and improve their long-term returns. By staying calm, identifying undervalued stocks, using dollar-cost averaging, rebalancing portfolios, and monitoring economic trends, investors can turn short-term declines into long-term gains.

Market corrections are not crashes—they are healthy resets that bring valuations back in line with fundamentals. Investors who recognize this reality gain a significant advantage over those who panic and sell. By embracing volatility as a tool for opportunity, investors can build wealth with confidence, regardless of market fluctuations.

6.2 How to Protect Your Portfolio During Market Downturns

Market downturns are inevitable, and while they can create buying opportunities, they can also lead to significant portfolio losses if investors are unprepared. Professional investors do not simply ride out market declines—they take strategic steps to minimize losses and protect their capital. Having a defensive strategy in place before a downturn occurs ensures that investors can navigate volatility with confidence while maintaining long-term investment success.

Understanding Market Downturns and Their Impact on Portfolios

A market downturn is a period when stock prices decline across a broad index like the S&P 500, Dow Jones, or Nasdaq. Downturns can range from mild corrections (-10%) to bear markets (-20% or more) and can last anywhere from a few weeks to several months or even years. The most severe downturns often coincide with economic recessions, where corporate earnings decline, unemployment rises, and consumer confidence weakens.

While market downturns cause fear among investors, they are a normal part of stock market cycles. Historically, the stock market has always recovered from downturns, with bull markets lasting much longer than bear markets. Investors who understand this historical perspective and prepare accordingly can avoid panic-driven decisions and position themselves for long-term gains.

Key Strategies to Protect Your Portfolio During a Downturn

Professional investors use a combination of risk management, diversification, defensive assets, and hedging techniques to minimize losses while keeping their portfolios positioned for future growth.

1. Diversify Across Sectors and Asset Classes

One of the most effective ways to protect a portfolio during a downturn is to ensure proper diversification. A well-diversified portfolio includes a mix of different asset classes and sectors that perform well in different market conditions.

- **Defensive sectors** – Industries like healthcare, consumer staples, and utilities tend to be more stable during downturns because people continue spending on essential goods and services.
- **Dividend stocks** – Companies with strong dividend histories provide steady income and tend to be more resilient in bear markets.
- **Bonds and fixed-income securities** – U.S. Treasury bonds, municipal bonds, and investment-grade corporate bonds offer stability when stock markets decline.
- **Commodities and precious metals** – Gold and silver often perform well when markets are volatile, as investors seek safe-haven assets.
- **Real estate investment trusts (REITs)** – REITs generate passive income from rental properties, which can provide stability when stock prices drop.

Example:

If an investor's portfolio is heavily concentrated in technology stocks, which tend to be volatile, they can balance risk by adding consumer staples (e.g., Procter & Gamble), utilities (e.g., Duke Energy), and healthcare stocks (e.g., Johnson & Johnson) to stabilize performance.

2. Adjust Asset Allocation Based on Market Conditions

While long-term investors should not try to time the market, adjusting asset allocation based on economic conditions can reduce downside risk.

In bull markets, investors may allocate more capital to growth stocks and cyclical industries that benefit from economic expansion.

In bear markets, shifting a portion of investments into cash, bonds, or defensive stocks helps preserve capital.

A common strategy is the 60/40 portfolio, where 60% is invested in stocks and 40% in bonds. During a downturn, an investor may temporarily shift to a 50/50 mix to reduce risk.

3. Keep a Cash Reserve for Buying Opportunities

Holding 5-15% of a portfolio in cash or cash equivalents provides liquidity to take advantage of discounted stock prices during downturns. Instead of panic selling, investors with cash reserves can buy high-quality stocks at lower prices, improving long-term returns.

Example:

During the COVID-19 market crash (March 2020), many stocks dropped 30-50%. Investors who had cash available were able to buy companies like Amazon, Apple, and Microsoft at bargain prices before they rebounded to new highs.

4. Use Stop-Loss Orders to Minimize Losses

A stop-loss order automatically sells a stock if it declines past a certain percentage, preventing further losses. This strategy is useful for protecting capital in high-volatility environments.

Types of Stop-Loss Strategies:

- **Fixed Percentage Stop-Loss** – Selling a stock if it drops by 15-20% to prevent further downside.
- **Trailing Stop-Loss** – Adjusting the stop-loss level as the stock price rises, locking in gains while limiting downside risk.

Example:

If an investor buys a stock at $100 per share and sets a 15% stop-loss, the stock will be automatically sold if it drops to $85, preventing further losses.

5. Hedge Your Portfolio with Defensive Investments

Hedging involves using alternative investments or financial instruments to protect a portfolio from significant losses.

Hedging Strategies:

- **Buying Put Options** – A put option increases in value when a stock price declines, acting as "insurance" against losses.
- **Inverse ETFs** – ETFs like SQQQ or SPXS rise when the market declines, helping offset portfolio losses.
- **Gold and Precious Metals** – These assets often perform well during market downturns as investors seek safe-haven investments.

Example:

An investor who owns $50,000 in S&P 500 stocks might buy $5,000 worth of SPXS (an inverse ETF) to partially hedge against market declines.

6. Rebalance the Portfolio to Maintain Proper Risk Levels

Market downturns can shift the balance of a portfolio, making certain assets overweight or underweight. Rebalancing ensures that risk levels remain controlled.

If stocks decline significantly, the portfolio may become overweight in bonds or cash.

If defensive assets increase in value, reallocating funds back into undervalued stocks improves long-term returns.

Rebalancing also prevents emotional decision-making by maintaining a structured investment approach.

Example:

If a portfolio was originally 70% stocks and 30% bonds, but after a market decline, it becomes 60% stocks and 40% bonds, rebalancing involves buying more stocks at lower prices to return to the 70/30 allocation.

7. Focus on Long-Term Investing and Avoid Panic Selling

The most important rule during a downturn is staying focused on long-term goals rather than reacting emotionally to short-term declines. Investors who sell during downturns often miss the recovery and lock in losses.

Historical Perspective:

- **The Great Recession (2008-2009):** The S&P 500 fell 50%, but investors who held on saw the market fully recover and reach new highs by 2013.
- **COVID-19 Crash (March 2020):** The market dropped 35%, but recovered in just five months, hitting record highs by the end of the year.

Patience is key—bear markets do not last forever. Those who stay invested and even buy more during downturns typically see higher long-term returns.

Preparing for Market Downturns with a Defensive Strategy

Market downturns are inevitable, but they do not have to be devastating. By implementing diversification, stop-loss strategies, cash reserves, hedging, and portfolio rebalancing, investors can minimize risk while positioning themselves for long-term success. Rather than fearing downturns, investors should view them as opportunities to buy quality stocks at lower prices and strengthen their portfolios. The key to surviving and thriving during market downturns is having a plan, managing emotions, and staying committed to long-term investment goals.

6.3 How to Stay Calm and Make Smart Decisions During Market Crashes

Market crashes are one of the most feared events in investing. They often trigger panic, emotional decision-making, and rushed selloffs, causing investors to lock in losses instead of positioning themselves for future gains. While crashes can be unsettling, they are not the end of the stock market—they are temporary disruptions that long-term investors can navigate successfully. Knowing how to stay calm, assess the situation logically, and make informed decisions can turn a market crash into an opportunity instead of a disaster.

Understanding Market Crashes and Their Causes

A market crash is a sudden and sharp decline in stock prices, usually by 20% or more in a brief period. Unlike normal corrections or downturns, crashes are often driven by panic, forced liquidations, or major economic events. Some of the most common causes of market crashes include:

- **Economic recessions** – A slowdown in GDP, rising unemployment, and declining corporate profits can trigger widespread selloffs.
- **Financial crises** – Events like the 2008 global fiscal crisis, which exposed weaknesses in the banking system, can cause steep declines.
- **Black swan events** – Unpredictable crises such as the COVID-19 pandemic can send shockwaves through global markets.
- **High speculation and asset bubbles** – When stocks become extremely overvalued (e.g., the dot-com bubble of 2000), markets eventually correct sharply.
- **Interest rate shocks** – Sudden increases in interest rates can reduce liquidity and make borrowing more expensive, leading to stock price declines.

While these events may cause temporary fear, history shows that every major market crash has eventually been followed by a recovery. Understanding this reality is crucial for maintaining composure during periods of extreme volatility.

How to Stay Calm During a Market Crash

When stock prices plummet, fear can drive investors to make irrational decisions. However, seasoned investors know that staying calm and sticking to a plan leads to better long-term outcomes. Here are key strategies to remain level-headed:

1. Remind Yourself That Crashes Are Temporary

Market crashes feel catastrophic in the moment, but history proves that they are always temporary. The stock market has survived numerous crashes, including:

- **The Great Depression (1929)** – The market eventually recovered and reached new highs.
- **The Black Monday Crash (1987)** – The Dow Jones fell 22% in a single day but rebounded within two years.
- **The Global Financial Crisis (2008-2009)** – The S&P 500 dropped 50%, but investors who stayed invested saw massive gains in the following decade.
- **The COVID-19 Crash (2020)** – Markets fell over 30% in a month but recovered to all-time highs within a year.

Each of these crashes seemed like the worst financial disaster at the time, yet the market eventually rebounded stronger than before. Reminding yourself of this long-term perspective can prevent panic-driven decisions.

2. Avoid Checking Your Portfolio Too Frequently

One of the biggest mistakes investors make during a crash is constantly checking their portfolios. Seeing daily losses increases anxiety and can push investors toward selling at the worst possible time. Instead of obsessing over short-term fluctuations, focus on your long-term investment goals.

A practical approach is to set specific review intervals—for example, only checking your portfolio once a week or once a month during volatile periods. This prevents emotional reactions and ensures that decisions are based on rational analysis rather than fear.

3. Focus on Fundamentals, Not Fear

Stock prices can fall sharply during a crash, but that does not mean the underlying businesses have lost value. Companies with strong fundamentals—consistent earnings, low debt, and competitive advantages—will survive and thrive after the crash. Instead of focusing on price movements, ask yourself:

Has the company's revenue or profit significantly declined?

Is the company still financially stable with a strong balance sheet?

Does the company have a durable competitive advantage?

If the answer to these questions is yes, then the stock's drop in price is temporary. Long-term investors should use crashes as opportunities to accumulate shares in fundamentally strong businesses at a discount.

4. Stick to Your Investment Plan

Before a crash occurs, every investor should have an investment plan with clear objectives, risk management strategies, and a defined asset allocation. When markets are crashing, refer to your plan instead of making impulsive decisions.

A strong investment plan includes:

- A diversified portfolio to limit downside risk.
- A long-term strategy that accounts for market cycles.
- Risk management rules (such as stop-loss limits or cash reserves).
- Guidelines for buying and selling decisions based on fundamentals, not emotions.

If your plan is well-structured, a market crash should not derail your long-term goals. Instead, it should be viewed as part of the normal investment journey.

5. Take Advantage of Buying Opportunities

While most investors panic and sell during a crash, smart investors see it as a chance to buy quality stocks at a discount. Some of the best investment opportunities arise when strong companies are temporarily undervalued due to fear-driven selling.

A good approach is to use dollar-cost averaging (DCA)—gradually investing at lower prices instead of trying to time the bottom.

Example:

If a stock were trading at $200 before the crash and drops to $150, an investor could buy lesser amounts at $150, $140, and $130, reducing their average cost per share while avoiding the risk of buying too early.

6. Avoid Selling Out of Fear

One of the worst mistakes investors make during market crashes is selling their stocks in panic, locking in losses that could have been recovered.

Historically, investors who sell during crashes often miss the best days of market rebounds. Studies show that missing just the 10 best trading days in a decade can reduce total returns by 50% or more.

Example:

An investor who stayed invested in the S&P 500 from 1990 to 2020 would have earned an average annual return of about 10%.

If they missed just the best 10 days of market rebounds, their return would have dropped to 5% or lower.

Selling during a crash means missing these crucial recovery periods, which can significantly impact long-term wealth accumulation.

7. Keep a Long-Term Perspective

Stock market crashes can be distressing, but they are only a problem if you need the money immediately. If you are investing for retirement or long-term wealth building, short-term volatility does not matter as much as your overall time horizon. The longer you stay invested, the higher your probability of success. Instead of worrying about a crash today, think about where the market will be in 5, 10, or 20 years.

Turning Market Crashes into an Advantage

Market crashes are challenging, but they are also opportunities for disciplined investors. By staying calm, avoiding emotional decisions, focusing on fundamentals, and sticking to a solid investment plan, investors can protect their portfolios and even capitalize on downturns. While the media often fuels fear during crashes, history shows that those who remain patient and continue investing emerge stronger. Instead of seeing a crash as a crisis, view it as a chance to accumulate quality assets at a discount and position yourself for long-term financial success.

CHAPTER 7 – THE PSYCHOLOGY OF SUCCESSFUL INVESTING

Investing is not just about numbers, financial models, or stock analysis—it is deeply influenced by psychology. The difference between successful and unsuccessful investors is often not their level of knowledge but rather how they manage their emotions, biases, and decision-making processes. Mastering the psychological aspects of investing is crucial for building long-term wealth, avoiding costly mistakes, and maintaining discipline through market cycles. Understanding how emotions drive market movements, recognizing cognitive biases, and developing a rational approach to investing can significantly improve financial outcomes.

The stock market is driven by human behaviour, and investor sentiment plays a key role in determining price movements. During periods of economic expansion and rising stock prices, optimism and greed take over, leading investors to take excessive risks, overpay for assets, and ignore warning signs of potential corrections. In contrast, during market downturns, fear and panic dominate, causing irrational selloffs, missed opportunities, and a general reluctance to invest when prices are at their lowest. Recognizing these psychological patterns allows investors to remain objective and make decisions based on logic rather than emotion.

One of the biggest challenges investors faces is the tendency to follow the herd. When markets are rising, it is tempting to buy stocks simply because others are doing the same, fearing the regret of missing profits. This behaviour leads to the creation of speculative bubbles, where stocks become overpriced due to mass enthusiasm rather than fundamental value. Similarly, during market crashes, panic selling becomes contagious, as investors rush to sell out of fear, causing stock prices to decline even further. The ability to resist herd mentality and think independently is one of the most valuable traits of successful investors.

Cognitive biases also play a significant role in investment decision-making. Confirmation bias leads investors to seek information that supports their existing beliefs while ignoring contradictory evidence. For example, an investor who is convinced that a particular stock will continue rising may only pay attention to positive news while disregarding warning signs of potential risks. Anchoring bias causes investors to fixate on past prices, assuming that a stock that was once priced higher will eventually return to that level, even if the company's fundamentals have deteriorated. Loss aversion makes investors more sensitive to losses than to gains, leading them to hold onto losing stocks for too long, hoping for a recovery, or sell winning stocks too early out of fear of losing profits.

Emotional control is essential for long-term success in investing. Markets go through cycles of euphoria and despair, and investors who can maintain a disciplined, rational approach during these fluctuations are more likely to achieve superior results. Developing a set of predefined rules for buying and selling stocks helps eliminate impulsive decision-making. Having a clear investment thesis, setting realistic expectations, and using risk management strategies such as stop-loss levels or portfolio diversification can reduce the influence of emotions on investment choices.

Patience is another critical factor in successful investing. The most reliable path to wealth creation in the stock market is through long-term compounding rather than short-term speculation. Many investors get caught up in the excitement of daily price movements, trying to time the market or chase the latest high-flying stocks. However, the most successful investors, such as Warren Buffett, emphasize the importance of holding quality investments for the long term, allowing compounding returns to work in their Favor. Understanding that wealth accumulates over decades rather than weeks or months helps investors stay committed to their strategies without being distracted by short-term noise.

Discipline is required not only in sticking to an investment plan but also in maintaining consistency in contributions. Regularly investing, regardless of market conditions, helps build wealth over time while reducing the risk of making poor timing decisions. Strategies such as dollar-cost averaging, where investors buy stocks at regular intervals regardless of price fluctuations, ensure that investments continue to grow systematically without being affected by short-term volatility.

Adaptability is also a key psychological trait of successful investors. Markets change, industries evolve, and new opportunities arise. Investors who remain flexible and open-minded can adjust their strategies as needed without becoming overly attached to past decisions. A willingness to learn from mistakes, analyse what went wrong, and refine investment approaches helps investors continuously improve their performance. Those who stubbornly stick to failing strategies or refuse to acknowledge new market realities often suffer losses.

Developing a mindset of resilience is crucial for navigating the inevitable difficulties of investing. Every investor experiences setbacks, whether through market crashes, stock declines, or missed opportunities. What separates successful investors from the rest is their ability to recover, learn, and move forward without letting past failures dictate future actions. A long-term perspective, combined with emotional stability, prevents temporary losses from becoming permanent mistakes.

The psychology of investing is as important as technical or fundamental analysis. Emotional discipline, cognitive awareness, patience, and adaptability are all critical components of long-term success in the stock market. By understanding how psychological factors influence investment decisions, investors can build strategies that minimize emotional mistakes, take advantage of market inefficiencies, and remain focused on long-term wealth creation. Mastering the psychological side of investing is what allows investors to turn market volatility into opportunity rather than fe

7.1 How to Develop a Winning Investor Mindset

Success in investing is not solely determined by financial knowledge, analytical skills, or access to market data. The most critical factor in achieving long-term wealth is the mindset of the investor. The way an individual thinks, reacts to market fluctuations, and manages uncertainty plays a crucial role in determining their financial success. Developing a winning investor mindset requires emotional discipline, strategic thinking, and the ability to stay focused on long-term goals despite short-term challenges.

One of the most important aspects of an investor's mindset is having a long-term perspective. The stock market is inherently volatile, with prices fluctuating daily based on economic reports, earnings releases, geopolitical events, and investor sentiment. However, history has consistently shown that markets rise over the long run. Investors who focus on long-term trends rather than short-term price movements tend to outperform those who constantly react to market noise. Instead of worrying about daily stock fluctuations, successful investors evaluate whether their investments align with their long-term financial goals and continue to show strong business fundamentals.

Patience is a key component of an investor's mindset. Many new investors expect to see immediate results and become frustrated when their stocks do not generate quick profits. However, wealth accumulation in the stock market occurs through compounding returns, which require time to take effect. The most successful investors understand that great companies may take years to deliver substantial gains. By resisting the urge to chase quick profits and instead allowing investments to grow, investors can benefit from exponential long-term returns. Warren Buffett, one of the greatest investors of all time, famously said, "The stock market is a device for transferring money from the impatient to the patient."

Another critical element of a winning investor mindset is the ability to control emotions during market fluctuations. Fear and greed are the two most powerful emotions that drive irrational decision-making. Fear causes investors to sell during market downturns, locking in losses instead of waiting for a recovery. Greed leads to reckless speculation, causing investors to buy overvalued stocks or take excessive risks. The best investors develop emotional resilience, remaining calm during bear markets and avoiding impulsive investments during bull markets. Practicing emotional detachment from stock price movements and making decisions based on logic rather than emotion is essential for long-term success.

One of the biggest psychological traps investors fall into is confirmation bias, the tendency to seek out information that supports existing beliefs while ignoring evidence that contradicts them. Investors who are overly confident in a stock may overlook red flags or warning signs, leading to poor investment decisions. To combat confirmation bias, investors should actively seek out contrarian opinions, analyse risks objectively, and consider multiple perspectives before making investment decisions. Remaining open-minded and willing to adjust strategies based on added information is a hallmark of successful investors.

Another common psychological bias that affects investors is loss aversion, the tendency to feel the pain of losses more intensely than the pleasure of gains. This bias often causes investors to hold onto losing stocks for too long, hoping they will recover rather than cutting losses early. Alternatively, some investors sell winning stocks too soon out of fear that profits will disappear. Recognizing loss aversion and making rational, data-driven decisions instead of emotional ones can significantly improve portfolio performance.

Discipline is another cornerstone of a successful investor's mindset. Many investors fail not because they lack knowledge, but because they lack the discipline to follow a structured investment plan. Developing a strategy that includes clear entry and exit rules, a well-defined asset allocation, and risk management protocols helps investors stay on course, even during market downturns. Sticking to a plan prevents emotional decision-making and ensures that investments are made based on long-term objectives rather than short-term impulses.

A winning investor mindset also includes a commitment to continuous learning. The financial markets are constantly evolving, and investors who remain curious, open to innovative ideas, and willing to refine their strategies will have a greater advantage. Reading financial books, following market trends, analysing economic indicators, and studying past investment successes and failures provide valuable insights that improve decision-making. The best investors treat investing as an ongoing learning process rather than a fixed set of rules.

Adaptability is another essential trait for long-term success in investing. Markets go through different cycles, and strategies that worked in one environment may not work in another. Investors who cling to outdated strategies or refuse to acknowledge changes in economic conditions often struggle to achieve consistent returns. Being flexible and adjusting investment strategies based on market conditions, emerging industries, and economic trends helps investors stay ahead of the curve.

Finally, resilience is crucial for maintaining a strong investor mindset. Every investor will experience setbacks, bad trades, or market downturns. The ability to recover from mistakes, analyse what went wrong, and move forward with confidence separates successful investors from those who give up. Accepting that losses are part of the investment process and learning from them allows investors to improve over time rather than becoming discouraged.

Developing a winning investor mindset requires patience, emotional discipline, adaptability, continuous learning, and the ability to think independently. By focusing on long-term goals, making data-driven decisions, and remaining resilient through market cycles, investors can increase their chances of achieving financial success. The stock market rewards those who approach investing with strategic thinking, a rational mindset, and the ability to remain calm in the face of uncertainty.

7.2 How to Overcome Psychological Biases That Hurt Your Investments

One of the biggest obstacles to successful investing is not the market itself, but the way our minds process investment decisions. Investors often believe that stock market success depends solely on picking the right stocks, timing the market, or following expert advice. However, psychological biases play a significant role in how we make investment decisions, often leading to mistakes that reduce long-term returns. Overcoming these biases is essential for making rational, disciplined, and effective investment choices.

Understanding Common Psychological Biases in Investing

Every investor, whether beginner or experienced, is influenced by cognitive biases. These biases lead to irrational behaviour, poor risk assessment, and emotional decision-making. Recognizing and managing these biases can improve decision-making, leading to better investment outcomes.

Confirmation Bias: The Trap of Seeking What We Want to Hear

Confirmation bias occurs when investors search for, interpret, or remember information in a way that confirms their existing beliefs, while ignoring evidence that contradicts them. If an investor believes a particular stock is a great buy, they may focus only on positive news while dismissing negative reports, leading to poor decision-making.

How to Overcome It:

Actively seek out contrarian viewpoints and negative reports about a stock before making an investment decision.

Follow structured research by analysing both bullish and bearish perspectives on a company.

Consider using checklists or scoring systems to evaluate stocks objectively rather than emotionally.

Example:

An investor is convinced that a tech stock will double in price. Instead of looking at potential risks like increasing competition, regulatory challenges, or slowing revenue growth, they only focus on analyst upgrades and ignore red flags. By considering opposing views, they might make a more balanced decision.

Loss Aversion: The Fear of Losing Money Leads to Bad Decisions

Loss aversion refers to the tendency of investors to feel the pain of losses more intensely than the joy of gains. This bias causes two major mistakes:

Holding onto losing stocks too long, hoping they will recover, even when the fundamentals are deteriorating.

Selling winning stocks too early, fearing that gains might disappear, rather than letting them grow.

How to Overcome It:

- Set predefined exit strategies for both profits and losses, avoiding emotional decision-making.
- Accept that losses are part of investing, and that no investor has a perfect track record.

- Use a stop-loss strategy to automatically sell a stock if it declines beyond a certain point.
- Keep a long-term perspective—just because a stock drops temporarily does not mean it is a failure.

Example:

An investor buys a stock at $100 per share. The price drops to $75, but instead of re-evaluating whether the company's fundamentals remain strong, they hold onto it just to avoid realizing a loss. Meanwhile, another investor sets a stop-loss at $85 and moves on to a better opportunity.

The Disposition Effect: Selling Winners and Holding Losers

The disposition effect is closely related to loss aversion. Investors often sell stocks that have gained value too early to "lock in profits," while holding onto losing stocks too long, hoping they will recover. This results in an unbalanced portfolio, where weak stocks remain while strong stocks are sold off too soon.

How to Overcome It:

- Reframe your mindset: think in terms of maximizing total portfolio returns, not individual stock performance.
- Regularly review portfolio performance and determine if each stock still meets your investment criteria.
- Recognize that just because a stock has gained value does not mean it has reached its full potential.

Example:

An investor buys Stock A at $50, and it rises to $75. Fearing that the gains might disappear, they sell it. Meanwhile, Stock B, which they bought at $50, drops to $30, but they refuse to sell because they do not want to admit a loss. Over time, Stock A continues rising to $150, while Stock B remains stagnant. The investor lost out on greater gains due to emotional decision-making.

Anchoring Bias: Fixating on Past Prices Instead of Current Value

Anchoring bias causes investors to focus too much on a stock's past price, if it traded at a certain level before, it would return to that level in the future. This can lead to bad investment decisions, such as buying a stock just because it has fallen from a previous high, without considering why it dropped.

How to Overcome It:

Base investment decisions on current fundamentals, not past price history.

Ask: ***"Would I buy this stock today based on its current financials, valuation, and outlook?"*** If the answer is no, do not hold onto it hoping for a rebound.

Focus on what the stock is worth today, not what it was worth six months ago.

Example:

A stock was trading at $200 last year but is now at $120. Investors assume it must "bounce back" to $200, even though the company's profits are declining, and competitors are taking market share. A rational investor would analyse whether the company is still fundamentally strong before assuming a price recovery.

Herd Mentality: Following the Crowd Instead of Thinking Independently

Many investors follow what others are doing instead of conducting independent research. This leads to buying stocks during market bubbles or selling in panic when everyone else is selling. Herd mentality drives stock market cycles of euphoria and fear, often leading to irrational price movements.

How to Overcome It:

- Develop independent thinking and invest based on research, not popular opinion.
- Avoid buying stocks simply because they are trending or frequently mentioned in financial media.
- Be willing to take contrarian positions if the data supports it.

Example:

During the dot-com bubble, many investors bought internet stocks just because everyone else was doing so, ignoring the fact that many of these companies were unprofitable. When the bubble burst, these investors suffered huge losses.

Meanwhile, those who remained disciplined and focused on fundamental investing avoided the crash.

Recency Bias: If Recent Trends Will Continue Indefinitely

Recency bias causes investors to overweight recent events and assume that past performance predicts future results. When stocks are rising, investors assume they will always rise. When the market is crashing, they assume it will never recover. This leads to poor timing decisions.

How to Overcome It:

- Look at long-term historical data rather than focusing on short-term movements.
- Remember that markets move in cycles—no stock goes up forever, and no bear market lasts indefinitely.
- Diversify across different asset classes to avoid overexposure to short-term trends.

Example:

An investor sees the S&P 500 rise 20% in one year and assumes it will continue at the same pace, investing everything in high-growth stocks. The following year, the market declines 15%, and they suffer major losses because they ignored the possibility of a correction.

Mastering Your Mindset for Better Investment Decisions

Psychological biases affect every investor, but those who recognize and control them make better decisions and achieve higher returns. By overcoming confirmation bias, loss aversion, the disposition effect, anchoring bias, herd mentality, and recency bias, investors can develop a rational, disciplined approach to investing. The best investors are not those who never make mistakes but those who learn from them and continuously refine their decision-making process. Investing is as much about managing your own psychology as it is about choosing stocks. By staying objective, focusing on fundamentals, and maintaining a long-term perspective, investors can avoid emotional traps and maximize their financial success

7.3 How to Build the Discipline and Patience Needed for Long-Term Investing Success

Investing success is not determined by intelligence, market timing, or stock-picking skills alone. The most important qualities of a successful investor are discipline and patience. These traits separate those who build long-term wealth from those who panic, trade impulsively, or give up when markets become volatile. Mastering the ability to stay invested, stick to a strategy, and make rational decisions despite market fluctuations is essential for achieving consistent financial growth.

Why Discipline and Patience Matter in Investing

The stock market does not move in a straight line. It experiences bull markets, bear markets, corrections, crashes, and recoveries. Investors who react emotionally to these cycles often make costly mistakes—buying high during euphoria and selling low during panic. History shows that the best returns come to those who stay invested through the difficulties, allowing time, and compounding to work in their Favor.

Many of the world's greatest investors, including Warren Buffett, emphasize the importance of patience. Buffett famously said, "The stock market is a device for transferring money from the impatient to the patient." Those who jump in and out of stocks, chase short-term trends, or sell too early often underperform those who simply buy strong companies and hold them for years. The key reason patience is essential is compound interest. When investments grow over time and reinvested profits generate additional returns, wealth increases exponentially. However, compounding only works if an investor allows time to do its job. Those who frequently buy and sell stocks disrupt the compounding process, reducing potential gains.

How to Develop Investment Discipline

Discipline means sticking to a strategy, avoiding emotional decisions, and following a structured plan, even when markets are volatile. Many investors struggle with discipline because they let fear, greed, or impatience drive their actions. Developing a system to control emotions and stay committed to long-term goals is crucial for investment success.

1. Create and Follow a Clear Investment Plan

An investor without a plan is likely to make impulsive decisions based on market fluctuations. A well-structured investment plan provides guidance and removes emotions from decision-making.

A solid investment plan should include:

- **Clear financial goals** – Define what you are investing for (retirement, wealth building, financial independence).
- **Time horizon** – Decide whether your investments are short-term (1-5 years), medium-term (5-10 years), or long-term (10+ years).
- **Risk tolerance** – Assess how much volatility you can manage without panic-selling.
- **Asset allocation strategy** – Determine what percentage of your portfolio will be in stocks, bonds, real estate, or alternative assets.
- **Buying and selling rules** – Establish criteria for when you will buy, hold, or sell a stock based on fundamental analysis rather than emotions.

By setting predefined rules, investors avoid reacting to short-term market noise and instead make rational, strategic decisions.

2. Automate Your Investing to Remove Emotion

One of the best ways to develop discipline is to automate investments so that decision-making is not affected by emotions. Automatic investing ensures that money is consistently put into the market, regardless of short-term conditions.

Dollar-cost averaging (DCA) is an effective strategy for automating investments. By investing a fixed amount at regular intervals (e.g., monthly), investors reduce the impact of market volatility and avoid trying to time the market. This method prevents hesitation during market downturns and ensures that investments continue to grow over time.

Example:

An investor decides to invest $500 every month in an S&P 500 index fund, regardless of market conditions. When the market is up, they buy fewer shares; when the market is down, they buy more shares at a discount. Over time, this approach leads to lower average purchase costs and stronger long-term returns.

3. Avoid Overtrading and Short-Term Speculation

Many investors feel the need to constantly trade to maximize profits, but frequent trading often leads to underperformance due to higher transaction costs, tax inefficiencies, and poor timing. The most successful investors focus on long-term growth rather than short-term price movements.

Studies show that investors who trade frequently tend to earn lower returns than those who buy and hold. The more an investor tries to "beat the market" through constant trading, the more likely they are to make mistakes driven by fear, greed, or speculation.

Solution: Stick to a long-term strategy by selecting high-quality investments and holding them for years rather than days or months. Instead of watching daily price movements, focus on whether a company's fundamentals remain strong and aligned with long-term goals.

4. Reframe Market Corrections as Opportunities, Not Threats

Many investors panic when markets decline, fearing that they will lose money. However, successful investors see downturns as opportunities to buy great companies at discounted prices.

Market corrections and bear markets are a natural part of stock market cycles, and those who invest during these periods often see the highest returns when the market recovers. Instead of fearing volatility, disciplined investors keep cash reserves available to take advantage of market declines.

Example:

During the 2008 fiscal crisis, stock prices plummeted, and many investors sold their portfolios in panic. However, those who remained patient and continued investing saw their portfolios recover and grow significantly over the next decade. The S&P 500, which had fallen to around 700 points in early 2009, rose to over 4,000 points by 2023.

A disciplined investor understands that the best time to buy is when others are fearful and that stock market downturns are temporary.

5. Set Realistic Expectations to Reduce Impatience

Impatience leads to frustration and poor decision-making. Many investors expect instant profits, believing that stocks should always go up quickly. However, true wealth accumulation takes years or even decades.

By setting realistic expectations—such as aiming for an 8-10% average annual return over time—investors can avoid frustration and stay committed to their strategy. The market will have strong years and weak years, but long-term investors benefit from staying the course.

6. Learn to Manage Fear and Greed

- Fear and greed are the two most dangerous emotions in investing.
- Fear causes investors to sell too soon during downturns, missing future recoveries.
- Greed causes investors to chase speculative trends, buying overhyped stocks at peak prices.

Discipline means controlling these emotions by sticking to a strategy rather than reacting impulsively. Keeping a journal of past investment decisions can help identify patterns of emotional behaviour and prevent repeating mistakes.

7. Regularly Review and Rebalance, But Do not Overreact

Successful investors periodically review their portfolios to ensure they remain aligned with their goals, but they do not overreact to short-term news or trends.

A disciplined review process includes:

- Checking fundamental changes in stocks rather than reacting to price movements.
- Rebalancing once or twice a year to maintain asset allocation.
- Adjusting strategies only when long-term trends shift, not based on daily headlines.

Discipline and Patience Are the Keys to Wealth Creation

Investing is not about making the right trade today—it is about staying the course for years and allowing compounding to do its job. The investors who succeed are not those who make the most trades or follow market trends, but those who stick to a structured plan, avoid emotional decisions, and remain patient through market cycles. By developing a long-term mindset, automating investments, avoiding frequent trading, using corrections as opportunities, and managing emotions, investors can achieve consistent financial growth while reducing stress and uncertainty. The stock market rewards those who approach investing with discipline, patience, and a rational decision-making framework

CHAPTER 8 – HOW TO CREATE A STRATEGY THAT FITS YOUR PERSONAL INVESTMENT GOALS

Every investor has unique financial goals, risk tolerance, and time horizons. There is no single "best" investing strategy—what works for one person may not be suitable for another. The key to long-term success in the stock market is developing a personalized investment strategy that aligns with your specific financial objectives, lifestyle, and risk profile. A well-defined strategy provides clarity, consistency, and discipline, ensuring that investment decisions are made based on a structured plan rather than emotions or short-term market trends.

Before creating an investment strategy, it is essential to define what you want to achieve. Some investors prioritize capital appreciation, aiming for high returns over time. Others seek income generation, focusing on dividends or passive cash flow. Some prefer capital preservation, prioritizing lower-risk investments that protect their wealth. Identifying your goals allows you to select the right approach and asset allocation to match your needs.

A critical component of any strategy is time horizon. Short-term investors, such as those saving for a major purchase within the next few years, require a more conservative approach, with lower exposure to volatile stocks. Long-term investors, such as those planning for retirement in 20 or 30 years, can afford to take on more risk in pursuit of higher returns. The longer your time horizon, the greater the benefit of compounding, allowing small investments to grow into substantial wealth over time.

Risk tolerance is another defining factor in building an investment strategy. Some investors are comfortable with significant market fluctuations and can manage short-term volatility for the possibility of higher returns. Others prefer stability and lower risk, even if it means sacrificing potential gains. Understanding how you react to market movements is essential in determining the right mix of assets in your portfolio. Those with a high-risk tolerance may focus more on growth stocks and emerging markets, while those with a minimal risk tolerance may favour dividend-paying stocks, bonds, and defensive sectors.

Once financial goals, time horizon, and risk tolerance are established, the next step is determining the type of investment approach that best suits your profile. The most common strategies include growth investing, value investing, dividend investing, index investing, and a balanced portfolio approach. Growth investing focuses on companies with high revenue and earnings expansion, often in the technology, healthcare, and e-commerce sectors. Value investing targets undervalued stocks trading below their intrinsic value, looking for solid companies that are temporarily out of Favor with the market. Dividend investing prioritizes stocks that generate passive income, ensuring steady cash flow even during market downturns. Index investing involves passively tracking market indices, providing broad diversification with minimal effort. A balanced portfolio combines different asset classes and investment styles, reducing overall risk while maintaining steady growth.

Asset allocation is the foundation of any investment strategy. The proportion of stocks, bonds, real estate, commodities, and alternative assets in a portfolio determines both risk and potential returns. Younger investors with long time horizons may allocate 80-90% to stocks and 10-20% to bonds or cash, maximizing growth potential. Those nearing retirement may shift toward a 60-40 stock-bond allocation, ensuring greater capital protection. Strategic rebalancing ensures that the portfolio remains aligned with its intended objectives, adjusting allocations periodically to maintain risk levels.

Diversification is a crucial element of risk management within an investment strategy. A well-diversified portfolio reduces dependence on a single stock, sector, or market, protecting against unexpected downturns. Diversification should occur across different industries, market capitalizations, and geographic regions. A portfolio composed solely of technology stocks is highly vulnerable to tech sector downturns, whereas a mix of technology, healthcare, consumer staples, energy, and financial stocks ensures greater stability. International diversification allows investors to benefit from global economic growth, spreading risk across different economies.

Regular portfolio monitoring and adjustments ensure that an investment strategy remains effective over time. While long-term investing emphasizes patience and discipline, occasional reviews help identify underperforming assets, changing economic conditions, and shifting personal financial needs. Investors should conduct quarterly or annual reviews, rebalancing portfolios when necessary and evaluating whether their investments still align with their original strategy.

A successful investment strategy also incorporates tax efficiency and cost management. Minimizing unnecessary taxes and expenses increases overall returns. Holding investments in tax-advantaged accounts (such as retirement funds or tax-deferred accounts) can reduce tax liabilities. Tax-loss harvesting strategies allow investors to offset capital gains by selling losing investments. Choosing low-cost index funds and ETFs instead of high-fee mutual funds helps reduce unnecessary expenses over time. Another vital component of an effective investment strategy is behavioural discipline. Investors must resist emotional decision-making, such as panic selling during downturns or chasing overhyped stocks during market booms. Sticking to a long-term plan, regardless of market fluctuations, is essential for success.

Developing a rational, objective approach prevents fear and greed from influencing investment decisions. The best investment strategy is one that fits your individual goals, risk tolerance, and financial situation. There is no single formula for success, but a structured, personalized approach ensures that your investments remain aligned with your objectives. By setting clear goals, defining risk tolerance, diversifying wisely, monitoring progress, and maintaining discipline, investors can create a long-term strategy that builds wealth and provides financial security.

8.1 How to Set Clear Investment Goals and Align Your Strategy for Success

Setting clear investment goals is the foundation of any successful strategy. Without a defined objective, investors often make impulsive decisions, chase short-term market trends, or take on unnecessary risks. A well-structured investment plan ensures that every decision aligns with long-term financial aspirations, balancing growth, stability, and risk management.

Understanding Why Investment Goals Matter

Investing without a goal is like driving without a destination. Without a clear purpose, it becomes difficult to measure progress, determine success, or make strategic adjustments when needed. Setting well-defined goals helps investors prioritize their financial needs, choose the right assets, and maintain focus during market fluctuations.

Well-established goals help prevent emotional decision-making. When markets are volatile, investors without a plan often react impulsively—panic selling during downturns or chasing overvalued stocks during bull markets. Having a clear financial roadmap keeps investors focused on their long-term objectives rather than short-term price movements.

Types of Investment Goals

Investment goals vary from person to person, depending on financial situation, age, risk tolerance, and time horizon. The most common investment objectives include:

- **Wealth Building for Long-Term Growth** – Investors seeking capital appreciation over decades focus on high-growth stocks, index funds, and diversified portfolios.
- **Generating Passive Income** – Those wanting consistent cash flow may prioritize dividend stocks, bonds, and real estate investment trusts (REITs).
- **Saving for Retirement** – Individuals planning for retirement invest in tax-advantaged accounts (IRAs, 401(k)s) and long-term growth assets.
- **Short-Term Financial Goals** – Some investors aim to save for specific short-term needs, such as buying a house, funding education, or starting a business.

Each goal requires a different strategy, asset allocation, and risk approach. The key is matching investments with the appropriate time horizon and financial objective.

How to Set Realistic and Achievable Investment Goals

To create effective investment goals, investors should follow the SMART framework:

- **Specific** – Clearly define what you want to achieve. Instead of saying, "I want to grow my money," specify, "I want to accumulate $500,000 for retirement by age 60."
- **Measurable** – Track progress with clear benchmarks, such as expected annual returns or portfolio milestones.
- **Achievable** – Set goals that align with realistic financial capabilities and risk tolerance.

- **Relevant** – Ensure that goals match long-term personal and financial needs.
- **Time-Bound** – Establish a timeframe for achieving each goal to maintain accountability.

Example:

- **Goal:** Save $1 million for retirement in 30 years.
- **Strategy:** Invest $1,000 per month into a diversified stock portfolio with an expected annual return of 8%.
- **Measurement:** Track portfolio growth annually to ensure alignment with projections.

Aligning Your Strategy with Your Investment Goals

Once goals are established, the next step is designing an investment strategy that aligns with those objectives. The risk level, asset allocation, and investment vehicles chosen should reflect the investor's time horizon and financial target.

1. Determining the Right Asset Allocation

The mix of stocks, bonds, real estate, and alternative investments should be structured according to risk tolerance and time horizon.

- **Short-Term Goals (1-5 Years)** – Conservative portfolios with high liquidity, lower volatility assets, such as bonds, cash, or short-term ETFs.
- **Medium-Term Goals (5-15 Years)** – Balanced portfolios with a mix of stocks and fixed-income assets to ensure growth while minimizing excessive risk.
- **Long-Term Goals (15+ Years)** – Growth-focused portfolios with higher exposure to stocks and equity-based funds to maximize returns over time.

Example of Asset Allocation for Different Investment Goals:

Investment Goal	Stocks	Bonds	Cash	Real Estate
Short-Term (Buying a house)	30%	50%	20%	0%
Medium-Term (Child's education in 10 years)	60%	30%	10%	0%
Long-Term (Retirement 30+ years)	80%	15%	5%	10%

This strategic asset allocation ensures that investments remain aligned with specific goals while managing risk appropriately.

2. Choosing the Right Investment Vehicles

Diverse types of investments serve different purposes. Selecting the right investment vehicles depends on the investor's goal:

- **For Long-Term Wealth Building** – Growth stocks, ETFs tracking the S&P 500, and emerging market funds.
- **For Passive Income** – Dividend-paying stocks, real estate (REITs), and bonds.
- **For Capital Preservation** – Treasury bonds, fixed-income securities, and money market funds.
- **For Tax Efficiency** – Retirement accounts (401(k), IRA) and tax-advantaged index funds.

Example:

If an investor's goal is to generate $50,000 per year in passive income, they could build a portfolio of high-yield dividend stocks and REITs, ensuring a steady stream of cash flow.

3. Implementing a Consistent Investment Plan

Once the strategy is defined, consistent execution is crucial. The best way to stay on track is to:

- **Invest regularly through dollar-cost averaging (DCA)** – Contributing a fixed amount each month ensures steady portfolio growth.
- **Rebalance periodically** – Adjusting allocations ensures that risk levels remain in line with original goals.
- **Monitor progress annually** – Evaluating portfolio performance prevents major deviations from targets.

Example of a Consistent Investment Plan:

- **Goal**: Retire with $2 million in 30 years.
- **Plan**: Invest $1,500 per month into a mix of S&P 500 ETFs, growth stocks, and dividend funds.
- **Adjustment:** Increase contributions when income rises or shift asset allocation based on market conditions.

Avoiding Common Mistakes When Setting Investment Goals

Many investors fail to achieve their goals due to common mistakes, including:

- **Lack of a clear plan** – Without structured objectives, investments lack direction.

- Unrealistic expectations – Expecting 20-30% annual returns leads to unnecessary risk-taking.
- **Ignoring risk tolerance** – Investing in volatile assets without considering personal risk capacity can cause panic selling.
- **Failure to adjust goals over time** – Life circumstances change, and investment strategies should adapt accordingly.

To avoid these pitfalls, investors should regularly review their financial objectives, reassess risk tolerance, and ensure that their portfolio remains aligned with long-term aspirations.

The Power of Goal-Based Investing

Setting clear investment goals provides structure, direction, and motivation to stay committed to a long-term financial plan. By aligning asset allocation, investment choices, and risk management with personal objectives, investors can maximize returns while maintaining stability. The key to success is not just choosing the right stocks but following a strategy tailored to individual financial needs, time horizons, and risk preferences. A well-defined investment goal acts as a roadmap, helping investors navigate market fluctuations and stay focused on long-term wealth creation. By staying disciplined, adjusting strategies as needed, and remaining patient, investors can ensure financial security and achieve their financial dreams.

8.2 How to Choose the Right Investment Strategy for Your Goals and Risk Tolerance

Every investor has unique financial goals, risk tolerance, and time horizons, making it essential to select an investment strategy that aligns with personal objectives. Choosing the right strategy can determine whether an investor successfully builds long-term wealth or struggles with market fluctuations. A well-structured approach ensures that investments are optimized for growth, income, or capital preservation while managing risk effectively.

Understanding Investment Strategies and Their Purpose

An investment strategy is a structured plan that guides how money is allocated across different asset classes, industries, and investment vehicles. Without a clear strategy, investors may chase trends, make emotional decisions, or take unnecessary risks, reducing their chances of long-term success. The key is selecting a strategy that matches financial goals and personal comfort with risk.

The right strategy should answer these fundamental questions:

- What is the primary investment goal? (e.g., long-term growth, passive income, or capital preservation)
- What is the preferred time horizon? (e.g., short-term, medium-term, or long-term)
- How much risk is acceptable? (e.g., conservative, moderate, or aggressive)
- How actively does the investor want to manage their portfolio? (e.g., passive investing vs. active stock selection)

By considering these factors, investors can develop a personalized investment approach that fits their financial needs.

Comparing the Most Common Investment Strategies

There are several proven investment strategies, each designed for different goals and risk tolerances. Choosing the right one requires understanding how they work, their benefits, and their risks.

1. Growth Investing (Best for Long-Term Capital Appreciation and High-Risk Tolerance)

Growth investing focuses on companies with above-average revenue and earnings growth, often in innovative industries such as technology, healthcare, and e-commerce. These companies reinvest profits to expand operations rather than paying dividends.

Characteristics:

- Invests in high-growth companies with strong future potential.
- Prioritizes capital appreciation over dividends or income.
- Typically involves higher volatility but greater long-term returns.

Who Should Use It?

- Investors with a long-time horizon (10+ years).
- Those comfortable with market fluctuations and short-term losses.
- People who want to maximize portfolio growth over time.

Example:

An investor using a growth strategy might focus on companies like Tesla, Amazon, and Nvidia, which have historically experienced strong revenue and earnings expansion.

2. Value Investing (Best for Long-Term Investors Looking for Undervalued Stocks)

Value investing seeks to buy stocks that are trading below their intrinsic value, often due to market mispricing, temporary issues, or negative sentiment. This strategy relies on fundamental analysis to identify companies that are financially strong but overlooked by the market.

Characteristics:

- Invests in undervalued companies with solid fundamentals.
- Emphasizes low price-to-earnings (P/E) ratios, strong balance sheets, and high return on equity (ROE).
- Aims for steady, long-term returns with less volatility than growth investing.

Who Should Use It?

- Investors with patience to wait for stock prices to recover.
- Those who prefer lower-risk investments with strong fundamentals.
- Investors comfortable with holding stocks for years until they reach fair value.

Example:

A value investor might buy stocks such as Coca-Cola, Johnson & Johnson, or Berkshire Hathaway when their prices dip below their historical valuation metrics.

3. Dividend Investing (Best for Passive Income and Moderate Risk Tolerance)

Dividend investing focuses on stocks that pay regular dividends, providing a steady stream of passive income while also offering capital appreciation potential.

Characteristics:

- Invests in established, profitable companies that return earnings to shareholders.
- Prioritizes stable and growing dividend payouts over time.
- Typically includes blue-chip stocks with lower volatility.

Who Should Use It?

- Investors looking for passive income for retirement or financial stability.
- Those who prefer steady returns rather than aggressive growth.
- Investors seeking lower risk and capital preservation.

Example:

Popular dividend stocks include Procter & Gamble, Johnson & Johnson, and Verizon, which have long histories of paying reliable dividends.

4. Index Fund Investing (Best for Passive Investors Who Want Broad Market Exposure)

Index investing involves buying exchange-traded funds (ETFs) or mutual funds that track a specific stock market index, such as the S&P 500 or Nasdaq. This strategy requires minimal effort and historically outperforms most actively managed funds over time.

Characteristics:

- Provides broad market diversification with minimal stock-picking effort.
- Typically has lower fees and fewer transaction costs.
- Delivers steady, long-term returns with reduced risk.

Who Should Use It?

- Investors who want a simple, low-maintenance approach.
- Those who prefer market-average returns without active management.
- People who are comfortable with long-term, passive investing.

Example:

An investor following this strategy might buy an ETF like VOO (Vanguard S&P 500 ETF) and hold it for decades without making frequent changes.

5. Balanced Portfolio Strategy (Best for Diversification and Risk Management)

A balanced portfolio strategy combines different asset classes, such as stocks, bonds, and real estate, to reduce overall risk. This approach helps investors weather market volatility while maintaining steady growth.

Characteristics:

- Diversifies across multiple asset classes to reduce risk.

- Provides moderate returns with lower volatility.
- Adjusts allocations based on market conditions and personal financial needs.

Who Should Use It?

- Investors who want a mix of growth and stability.
- Those nearing retirement who needs capital preservation.
- Investors with moderate risk tolerance.

Example of a Balanced Portfolio:

Asset Class	Allocation (%)
Stocks (Growth & Value)	50%
Bonds (Government & Corporate)	30%
Real Estate (REITs)	10%
Cash & Alternatives	10%

This portfolio provides both growth and stability, making it ideal for investors who want diversification without excessive risk.

How to Select the Right Strategy for Your Needs

To determine the best investment strategy, consider the following:

- **Define Your Financial Goals** – Do you want growth, passive income, or risk reduction?
- **Assess Your Risk Tolerance** – Can you manage volatility, or do you prefer stability?
- **Evaluate Your Time Horizon** – Are you investing for retirement in 30 years or a major expense in 5 years?
- **Decide on Active vs. Passive Investing** – Do you want to actively manage your portfolio or invest with minimal effort?
- **Consider Diversification Needs** – Would a mix of asset classes better suit your financial situation?

For beginners, a passive index fund strategy is often the best choice due to its simplicity and long-term reliability. For experienced investors, combining growth, value, and dividend investing can optimize portfolio performance.

Matching the Right Strategy to Your Investment Profile

There is no one-size-fits-all approach to investing. The best strategy depends on an investor's financial goals, risk tolerance, time horizon, and willingness to manage their portfolio. By understanding the advantages and risks of each approach, investors can create a customized investment plan that balances growth, stability, and income generation. A well-chosen investment strategy provides structure, reduces emotional decision-making, and increases the probability of long-term financial success.

8.3 How to Adapt Your Investment Strategy to Different Market Conditions

Markets are constantly changing, influenced by economic cycles, interest rates, inflation, and global events. A strategy that works in a bull market may not be effective in a bear market. Investors who adapt their investment strategy based on market conditions can protect their capital, minimize losses, and take advantage of new opportunities. Successful investors are not those who predict the market but those who adjust their approach based on changing conditions while staying committed to long-term goals.

Understanding Market Cycles and Their Impact on Investing

The stock market follows cycles of expansion and contraction, and recognizing these phases helps investors make better asset allocation decisions. The four main market conditions are:

- **Bull Market (Economic Expansion)** – Stock prices are rising, corporate earnings are strong, and investor confidence is high.
- **Market Correction (-10% Drop from Highs)** – A temporary pullback in stock prices that is often short-lived.
- **Bear Market (Economic Contraction, -20% Drop or More)** – Stock prices decline significantly, often due to economic downturns or crises.
- **Recovery Phase (Economic Rebound)** – The market stabilizes and begins growing again after a bear market.

Each phase presents unique challenges and opportunities. Investors who understand how to adjust their strategies accordingly can navigate market volatility more effectively.

How to Invest During a Bull Market

A bull market is characterized by rising stock prices, strong economic growth, and investor optimism. In this environment, investors should focus on capital appreciation and growth opportunities while managing risk appropriately.

Key Strategies:

- **Invest in Growth Stocks** – Companies with strong earnings growth, such as those in technology, healthcare, and consumer discretionary sectors, tend to outperform.
- **Increase Equity Exposure** – Since the market is rising, maintaining a higher percentage of stocks in the portfolio allows for greater upside.
- **Reduce Cash Holdings** – Keeping too much cash on the sidelines may lead to missed opportunities for growth.
- **Use Momentum Strategies** – Stocks with strong upward trends tend to continue performing well in bull markets.

Example:

During the bull market from 2009 to early 2020, technology stocks like Apple, Amazon, and Microsoft saw exponential growth. Investors who focused on high-growth sectors benefited the most.

Risk Management Tip:

Although bull markets can be exciting, it is important to avoid overconfidence and excessive risk-taking. Market euphoria can lead to bubbles, where investors pay too much for overvalued stocks.

How to Adjust During a Market Correction

Market corrections—declines of 10% or more—are a normal part of investing. They create uncertainty but also opportunities to buy quality stocks at lower prices.

Key Strategies:

- **Identify High-Quality Stocks on Sale** – Corrections often drag down strong companies along with weaker ones, creating buying opportunities.
- **Use Dollar-Cost Averaging (DCA)** – Investing in small increments reduces the risk of buying at the wrong time.
- **Hold a Cash Reserve** – Keeping cash available allows investors to take advantage of discounted prices.

- **Avoid Panic Selling** – Many investors sell during corrections out of fear, only to regret it when the market rebounds.

Example:

In early 2018, the market saw a correction of 10%, causing fear among investors. However, those who bought during the dip saw strong gains in the following months as the market quickly recovered.

Risk Management Tip:

During corrections, focus on long-term fundamentals rather than short-term price movements. Corrections are temporary and often lead to new highs.

How to Protect Your Portfolio During a Bear Market

A bear market is a prolonged downturn of 20% or more, often lasting months or years. These declines are usually driven by economic recessions, financial crises, or external shocks.

Key Strategies:

- **Increase Exposure to Defensive Stocks** – Sectors like healthcare, consumer staples, and utilities tend to hold up better in bear markets.
- **Add Dividend Stocks** – Companies with consistent dividend payouts provide income even when stock prices decline.
- **Hold Bonds and Fixed Income Assets** – Bonds are less volatile than stocks and can provide stability.
- **Use Hedging Strategies** – Investors can hedge risk by using put options, inverse ETFs, or commodities like gold.

Example:

During the 2008 fiscal crisis, defensive stocks like Procter & Gamble, Johnson & Johnson, and Coca-Cola outperformed the broader market. Investors who shifted to safe-haven assets avoided deeper losses.

Risk Management Tip:

It is important not to go entirely to cash, as bear markets eventually end. Staying partially invested ensures participation in the recovery phase.

How to Take Advantage of a Market Recovery

The recovery phase follows a bear market and presents some of the best opportunities for investors. As economic conditions improve, stock prices begin rising again.

Key Strategies:

- **Buy Growth Stocks Before They Rebound** – Companies that suffered the most during the downturn often recover the fastest.
- **Increase Exposure to Cyclical Stocks** – Sectors like technology, industrials, and financials perform well as economic confidence returns.
- **Rebalance the Portfolio** – Shift allocations back to a more aggressive growth strategy as market conditions improve.
- **Stay Invested to Capture Gains** – Many investors remain fearful after a bear market, missing recovery rallies.

Example:

After the COVID-19 crash in March 2020, the market rebounded quickly, with stocks like Tesla, Nvidia, and Amazon posting record gains. Investors who bought during the downturn saw massive returns.

Risk Management Tip:

Investors should look for early signals of economic recovery, such as:

- Rising corporate earnings
- Stronger GDP growth
- Decreasing unemployment rates

How to Balance Long-Term Investing with Short-Term Adjustments

While adapting to market conditions is important, investors should not abandon their long-term strategy every time the market shifts. The key is making small adjustments while maintaining a core portfolio strategy.

- **Avoid Trying to Time the Market** – No one can predict market tops and bottoms with certainty.
- **Maintain a Diversified Portfolio** – Holding different asset classes reduces overall risk.

- **Use a Core-Satellite Approach** – Keep a core portfolio of long-term holdings, while using smaller satellite investments for tactical adjustments.
- **Stay Disciplined** – Stick to an investment plan and avoid emotional trading based on fear or greed.

Example of Core-Satellite Portfolio Approach:

Investment Type	Allocation (%)
Core Holdings (Index Funds, Blue-Chip Stocks)	70%
Growth Stocks (Tech, Emerging Markets)	15%
Defensive Stocks (Healthcare, Consumer Staples)	10%
Alternative Investments (Gold, Bonds, Crypto)	5%

This approach ensures long-term stability while allowing flexibility to adapt to market trends.

Smart Investing Requires Flexibility and Discipline

Markets will always go through bull cycles, corrections, bear markets, and recoveries. The key to long-term success is not predicting these cycles but adjusting investment strategies accordingly. By investing in growth stocks during bull markets, holding defensive assets in bear markets, taking advantage of corrections, and capitalizing on recoveries, investors can navigate all market conditions successfully. The most successful investors combine patience, strategic adjustments, and a focus on long-term financial goals, ensuring consistent growth while managing risk.

CHAPTER 9 – HOW TO BUILD A PORTFOLIO THAT GROWS AND PROTECTS YOUR WEALTH

Creating a stock portfolio that balances growth and risk management is the key to long-term financial success. Many investors either take on too much risk in pursuit of high returns or are overly conservative, limiting their potential for growth. The most effective portfolios are structured to provide steady appreciation while safeguarding against market downturns. A well-built portfolio ensures financial stability, long-term wealth accumulation, and the ability to withstand economic fluctuations.

The Foundations of a Strong Portfolio

A successful investment portfolio is more than just picking good stocks. It requires a clear structure, diversification, and a disciplined approach to asset allocation. The goal is to create a portfolio that:

- Generates consistent returns over time.
- Minimizes risk through diversification.
- Balances growth stocks, income-generating assets, and defensive investments
- Adapts to changing market conditions without excessive trading.

The challenge many investors face is determining how to allocate their money effectively. Too much risk can lead to large losses, while excessive caution can lead to missed opportunities. The right balance depends on individual goals, risk tolerance, and investment timeline.

Step 1: Defining Your Investment Goals

Before building a portfolio, it is crucial to determine what you want to achieve. Different objectives require different investment strategies. The three most common investment goals are:

- **Long-Term Growth** – Maximizing capital appreciation over 10+ years (e.g., retirement savings, wealth building).
- **Passive Income** – Creating a steady stream of dividends or interest payments (e.g., financial independence, income replacement).
- **Capital Preservation** – Protecting wealth while maintaining moderate growth (e.g., saving for a house, minimizing risk).

Each of these goals influences asset allocation and stock selection. Investors seeking long-term growth may focus more on equities, while those prioritizing capital preservation allocate more to bonds and defensive assets.

Step 2: Choosing the Right Asset Allocation

Asset allocation refers to how an investor divides their portfolio among different asset classes, such as stocks, bonds, real estate, and alternative investments. The right mix depends on:

- Risk tolerance (How much volatility can you manage?)
- Time horizon (How long can you let your investments grow?)
- Income needs (Do you need regular cash flow, or can you reinvest profits?)

A growth-focused portfolio for a younger investor might include:

Asset Class	Allocation (%)
Growth Stocks	60%
Dividend Stocks	20%
Bonds & Fixed Income	10%
Alternative Assets (Real Estate, Commodities)	10%

A more conservative portfolio for an investor nearing retirement might look like this:

Asset Class	Allocation (%)
Dividend Stocks	40%
Bonds & Fixed Income	40%
Alternative Assets (Real Estate, Commodities)	15%
Cash & Cash Equivalents	5%

By diversifying across different asset classes, investors reduce risk while ensuring their portfolio continues to grow.

Step 3: Selecting the Right Stocks and Investments

Once asset allocation is determined, the next step is choosing high-quality investments that align with your financial goals. A well-balanced stock portfolio includes:

- **Growth Stocks** – Companies with strong earnings growth potential (e.g., technology, healthcare).
- **Dividend Stocks** – Reliable companies that pay consistent dividends (e.g., consumer staples, utilities).
- **Defensive Stocks** – Businesses that perform well in downturns (e.g., healthcare, essential services).
- **Blue-Chip Stocks** – Established, financially strong companies (e.g., Apple, Microsoft).

The key is to blend these categories so that different stocks provide stability, income, and capital appreciation.

Example Portfolio for a Balanced Growth Approach:

Stock Type	% Allocation	Example Stocks
Growth Stocks	50%	Amazon, Nvidia, Google
Dividend Stocks	30%	Johnson & Johnson, Procter & Gamble
Defensive Stocks	10%	Walmart, Coca-Cola
International Stocks	10%	Alibaba, Nestlé

Step 4: Managing Portfolio Risk

Even the best portfolios require risk management to withstand market downturns. The most effective ways to protect a portfolio include:

- **Diversification** – Holding different asset classes and sectors reduces exposure to any single risk.
- **Position Sizing** – Avoid concentrating too much money in a single stock or sector.
- **Stop-Loss Orders** – Setting automatic sell points prevents significant losses in market downturns.
- **Hedging with Bonds and Gold** – These assets often perform well when stock markets decline.

Investors should regularly review their portfolios and adjust allocations as needed. If one stock or sector grows too large, rebalancing ensures that risk remains controlled.

Step 5: Monitoring and Adjusting Your Portfolio

A great portfolio is not set and forget. Investors should monitor their holdings regularly, adjusting for market changes and personal financial goals.

- **Quarterly Reviews** – Check performance and sector exposure.
- **Annual Rebalancing** – Adjust allocations if one asset class has grown too large.
- **Economic Trend Monitoring** – Shift strategies based on interest rates, inflation, or global events.

For example, if technology stocks become overvalued, reducing exposure, and shifting capital to undervalued sectors (such as healthcare or energy) ensures better diversification.

Step 6: Avoiding Common Portfolio Mistakes

Many investors make costly errors when managing their portfolios. The most common mistakes include:

- **Overconcentration** – Investing too much in a single stock or sector increases risk.
- **Ignoring Market Conditions** – Failing to adjust to interest rate changes or economic shifts.

- **Emotional Decision-Making** – Buying at market highs and selling at lows due to fear or greed.
- **Chasing Hot Stocks** – Investing in speculative assets without understanding fundamentals.
- **Neglecting Portfolio Reviews** – Holding onto underperforming stocks for too long.

Avoiding these mistakes helps ensure a portfolio remains well-balanced and continues growing over time.

Step 7: Building a Portfolio for Long-Term Success

A strong portfolio is one that is:

- Well-diversified across different sectors and asset classes.
- Designed to match your personal risk tolerance and financial goals.
- Built with high-quality stocks, ETFs, and income-generating assets.
- Managed with a disciplined approach, avoiding emotional decision-making.
- Regularly reviewed and adjusted to stay aligned with market conditions.

The best investors stay patient, remain consistent, and avoid chasing trends. Wealth is built over time through smart asset allocation, disciplined investing, and strong risk management.

Your Portfolio is Your Financial Future

A well-structured investment portfolio provides the foundation for long-term financial security, growth, and wealth preservation. By setting clear goals, maintaining a diversified approach, and regularly monitoring investments, investors can build a portfolio that withstands market cycles while continuing to grow steadily. The key to success is discipline, patience, and a structured investment strategy. Those who stick to a well-defined plan, avoid emotional decision-making, and invest for the long run are the ones who achieve financial independence and wealth accumulation over time.

9.1 How to Diversify Your Portfolio to Maximize Returns and Minimize Risk

Diversification is one of the most powerful principles in investing. It protects portfolios from excessive risk while ensuring steady growth across different market conditions. A well-diversified portfolio allows investors to participate in various sectors, industries, and asset classes, reducing exposure to any single company or economic trend. Without diversification, portfolios become vulnerable to sharp declines when individual investments underperform. Investors who spread their capital across multiple assets can achieve more stable returns while mitigating the impact of market volatility.

The goal of diversification is not just to own multiple stocks but to construct a portfolio that balances risk and reward across different investments. Many investors mistakenly believe that owning several stocks within the same industry is sufficient diversification. However, if all holdings belong to a single sector, such as technology, the portfolio remains exposed to sector-specific downturns. True diversification involves selecting investments from different asset classes, industries, geographical regions, and market capitalizations, ensuring that losses in one area can be offset by gains in another.

One of the most effective ways to diversify a portfolio is by investing across multiple asset classes. Equities provide capital appreciation, but they also come with volatility. Bonds offer stability and predictable income, making them an essential component for balancing risk. Real estate investments, either through direct ownership or real estate investment trusts (REITs), provide inflation protection and income generation. Commodities such as gold and silver function as hedges during economic uncertainty, while alternative assets like private equity or cryptocurrency can offer additional growth opportunities.

Sector diversification is another critical element in reducing risk. The stock market is divided into various sectors, each influenced by different economic forces. Technology stocks thrive during economic expansion, while consumer staples and utilities perform well during recessions. Healthcare stocks remain resilient regardless of economic cycles, while financial stocks benefit from rising interest rates. A well-balanced portfolio allocates capital across multiple sectors to ensure stability throughout changing economic conditions.

Market capitalization diversification further strengthens portfolio resilience. Large-cap stocks provide stability and consistent returns due to their established market positions and reliable earnings. Mid-cap stocks offer a balance of growth and risk, often outperforming large caps during economic recoveries. Small-cap stocks carry higher volatility but also greater potential for rapid appreciation. By including companies of many sizes, investors gain exposure to various levels of risk and reward.

Geographical diversification reduces dependence on a single economy. Many investors concentrate their holdings in their home country, limiting their portfolio's growth potential. International diversification allows investors to benefit from economic expansion in different regions. Developed markets such as the United States and Europe offer stability, while emerging markets in Asia and Latin America present higher growth opportunities. Exposure to global equities ensures that portfolios remain resilient to economic downturns in any one country.

Another important aspect of diversification is choosing investments with low correlation. Correlation measures how assets move in relation to each other. Highly correlated assets tend to move in the same direction, increasing risk exposure. A portfolio composed solely of technology stocks will experience sharp declines if the tech sector crashes. However, if a portfolio includes a mix of growth stocks, dividend-paying stocks, bonds, and commodities, losses in one asset class may be offset by gains in another. Low correlation enhances portfolio stability, allowing investors to achieve consistent returns with reduced volatility.

Regular rebalancing is necessary to maintain diversification.

Over time, certain investments may outperform others, leading to an unbalanced portfolio. For example, if technology stocks surge while bonds remain stable, the portfolio may become overly concentrated in equities, increasing risk exposure. Rebalancing involves selling overperforming assets and reallocating funds to underperforming areas, ensuring that the portfolio stays aligned with the original investment strategy. This disciplined approach prevents excessive risk-taking and maintains long-term stability.

Investors must also be mindful of over-diversification. While diversification reduces risk, holding too many investments can dilute returns and make portfolio management difficult. Owning hundreds of stocks or investing in too many funds may lead to unnecessary complexity without significant benefits. The key is to strike a balance between spreading risk and maintaining a manageable number of high-quality investments.

A properly diversified portfolio does not eliminate risk entirely, but it does minimize the impact of market downturns while maximizing growth potential. The strongest portfolios include a mix of asset classes, industries, market capitalizations, and geographical regions, ensuring resilience across different economic cycles. By understanding the principles of diversification and implementing them strategically, investors can build portfolios that provide consistent returns and long-term financial security.

9.2 How to Rebalance Your Portfolio for Long-Term Stability and Growth

Portfolio rebalancing is a crucial aspect of investment management that ensures long-term stability while optimizing returns. Over time, market fluctuations cause asset allocations to drift from their original targets, leading to imbalances that can increase risk or reduce potential gains. By rebalancing periodically, investors maintain a diversified portfolio that aligns with their financial goals, risk tolerance, and time horizon. The process involves systematically adjusting asset allocations by selling overperforming investments and reinvesting in underweighted areas, bringing the portfolio back to its intended structure.

One of the main reasons to rebalance is risk management. A well-diversified portfolio is structured to balance growth and protection based on an investor's specific objectives. However, when certain assets outperform, they may become an oversized portion of the portfolio, increasing exposure to market volatility. For example, if technology stocks experience significant gains, their weight in the portfolio may rise from an initial 40% allocation to 60%. This imbalance exposes the investor to higher volatility and sector-specific risks. Rebalancing by selling a portion of these overgrown holdings and reallocating to undervalued sectors restores the portfolio's intended risk level.

Another key benefit of rebalancing is capitalizing on market inefficiencies. Markets move in cycles, with some asset classes or sectors becoming overvalued while others are temporarily undervalued. By periodically selling assets that have surged in price and reinvesting in those that are underperforming but still fundamentally strong, investors follow a disciplined "buy low, sell high" strategy. This approach enhances long-term returns by taking profits from overvalued assets and reinvesting in opportunities with higher growth potential.

Rebalancing frequency depends on individual preferences and market conditions. Some investors choose calendar-based rebalancing, adjusting their portfolios at set intervals such as quarterly, semi-annually, or annually. Others use threshold-based rebalancing, where adjustments are made only when an asset's allocation deviates beyond a specific percentage. For example, an investor may decide to rebalance whenever an asset class moves more than 5% away from its target allocation. Combining both methods ensures a structured approach while allowing flexibility based on market conditions.

Executing rebalancing efficiently requires careful planning to minimize transaction costs and tax implications. Selling assets to rebalance a portfolio can trigger capital gains taxes, particularly for investments held in taxable accounts. To reduce tax liabilities, investors can use tax-efficient rebalancing strategies, such as prioritizing adjustments within tax-advantaged accounts like IRAs or 401(k)s, where gains are deferred or exempt. Another approach is tax-loss harvesting, where investors sell underperforming assets at a loss to offset taxable gains from overperforming investments, lowering their overall tax burden.

Investors should also consider rebalancing in response to significant life events or changes in financial goals. If an investor approaches retirement, they may want to gradually shift their portfolio from aggressive growth stocks toward more stable income-producing assets such as bonds and dividend stocks. Similarly, if personal risk tolerance changes due to a shift in financial circumstances, adjusting asset allocations ensures that the portfolio remains aligned with new objectives. Automated rebalancing tools and robot-advisors can help streamline the process for those who prefer a hands-off approach. Many investment platforms offer automatic rebalancing services, ensuring portfolios remain properly allocated without requiring manual intervention. This feature is especially useful for passive investors who want to maintain diversification without actively managing their portfolio.

A well-balanced portfolio is the foundation of long-term financial success, and regular rebalancing helps maintain its integrity. By systematically adjusting asset allocations, investors reduce risk, enhance returns, and ensure their portfolio remains aligned with their evolving financial needs. Instead of reacting emotionally to market fluctuations, rebalancing enforces a disciplined investment strategy that promotes stability and sustained growth over time.

9.3 How to Protect Your Portfolio from Market Downturns and Economic Crises

Market downturns and economic crises are inevitable. Whether caused by recessions, financial crashes, geopolitical instability, or inflation spikes, these events create uncertainty and can lead to sharp declines in stock prices. Many investors panic during such periods, making emotional decisions that result in heavy losses. However, a well-structured portfolio, combined with proactive risk management strategies, can protect wealth, and ensure long-term stability. Successful investors focus on minimizing losses, maintaining diversification, and seizing opportunities during market declines rather than reacting impulsively to short-term volatility.

One of the most effective ways to safeguard a portfolio is diversification across asset classes, sectors, and geographical regions. A portfolio heavily concentrated in a single sector or country is vulnerable to downturns affecting that area. For example, during the 2008 fiscal crisis, banking and real estate stocks collapsed, but investors with holdings in consumer staples, healthcare, and government bonds experienced smaller losses. A diversified portfolio spreads risk by including growth stocks, defensive stocks, bonds, commodities, and alternative investments, ensuring that a decline in one asset class does not wipe out an investor's entire portfolio.

Holding defensive stocks and income-generating assets provides additional protection during downturns. Defensive sectors, such as consumer staples, healthcare, and utilities, tend to remain stable regardless of economic conditions because people continue spending on essential goods and services. Dividend-paying stocks offer a steady income stream, helping investors offset market declines by receiving cash flow even when stock prices fall. During bear markets, companies with strong balance sheets, low debt levels, and consistent earnings outperform speculative high-growth stocks, which are more vulnerable to downturns. Maintaining a cash reserve or liquidity buffer is essential for weathering economic crises. Investors who are fully invested in stocks may be forced to sell at a loss during downturns if they need access to cash. Keeping 5-15% of a portfolio in cash or short-term bonds ensures liquidity for emergencies while also providing funds to buy undervalued stocks at discounted prices when markets recover. Having available capital during a market crash allows investors to seize opportunities instead of panic selling. Another powerful risk management tool is asset allocation adjustments based on market conditions. During bull markets, an investor may hold a larger percentage of equities to maximize growth.

However, as warning signs of an economic slowdown appear—such as rising interest rates, slowing GDP growth, or increased market volatility—adjusting the portfolio to include more bonds, defensive stocks, and cash can reduce downside risk. Tactical allocation does not mean attempting to time the market but rather adjusting risk exposure based on economic indicators.

Investors can also use hedging strategies to protect their portfolios. One common approach is investing in gold and precious metals, which historically perform well during economic crises and inflationary periods. Another method is using inverse ETFs or put options, which gain value when the stock market declines. While hedging should not replace core investments, it can serve as a short-term shield during heightened volatility. Avoiding emotional decision-making is critical during downturns. Many investors sell at the bottom of a crash due to fear, missing the recovery.

Historically, bear markets have been followed by strong rebounds, and those who remain invested benefit from long-term gains. Reviewing historical data from past crises, such as the 2008 fiscal crisis or the COVID-19 market crash of 2020, demonstrates that markets eventually recover and reach new highs. The key is maintaining a disciplined approach and not letting short-term panic dictate long-term investment decisions.

Regularly rebalancing a portfolio during downturns ensures that allocations remain aligned with financial goals. If stocks decline significantly while bonds or cash positions increase in value, rebalancing by shifting funds back into equities at lower prices takes advantage of market inefficiencies. This disciplined approach prevents an investor from becoming overly defensive and missing recovery opportunities. Investors should also monitor macroeconomic indicators that signal potential downturns, such as rising inflation, declining corporate earnings, or central bank policy changes. Understanding these signals allows for proactive adjustments rather than reactive decisions. While predicting market crashes is impossible, recognizing risk factors helps investors prepare and adjust their portfolios accordingly.

A well-protected portfolio is built on a foundation of diversification, defensive assets, liquidity management, hedging strategies, and emotional discipline. Economic crises are part of investing, but they do not have to lead to financial ruin. By staying invested, making strategic adjustments, and maintaining a long-term perspective, investors can navigate downturns successfully and position themselves for future gains when markets recover.

CHAPTER 10 – MASTERING THE ART OF LONG-TERM INVESTING FOR LASTING WEALTH

Long-term investing is the most reliable path to building sustainable wealth and achieving financial independence. While short-term traders seek quick profits through market timing and speculation, the most successful investors—Warren Buffett, Charlie Munger, and Peter Lynch—have built their fortunes through discipline, patience, and a deep understanding of market fundamentals. The ability to hold investments over decades, navigate market cycles, and allow compounding to work its magic separates those who achieve financial success from those who chase short-term gains.

Many investors underestimate the power of compounding returns, which is often called the "eighth wonder of the world." Compounding allows investments to grow exponentially over time, as returns generate additional returns. A simple example illustrates this: An initial investment of $10,000 earning 8% annually will grow to $21,589 in 10 years, $46,610 in 20 years, and $100,627 in 30 years without any additional contributions. This principle is the foundation of long-term wealth creation and is why investors should prioritize time in the market over timing the market.

One of the biggest mistakes investors make is trying to time the market, believing they can predict market tops and bottoms. History proves that even the most experienced traders fail at consistently timing price movements. Studies show that missing just the 10 best days in the market over a 20-year period can cut overall returns in half. Instead of attempting to jump in and out of stocks based on news cycles, economic reports, or short-term volatility, successful investors remain fully invested in high-quality assets for the long haul.

The foundation of long-term investing is buying high-quality companies with durable competitive advantages. These businesses, often referred to as having economic moats, possess characteristics that protect them from competition and allow them to grow earnings steadily over time. Companies with strong brand recognition, pricing power, loyal customers, and consistent revenue streams tend to outperform overall. Investors should seek businesses with sustainable profit margins, high returns on capital, and a track record of innovation.

Understanding valuation and intrinsic value is also crucial for long-term success. Buying stocks at any price does not guarantee returns; investors must ensure they are purchasing great companies at reasonable valuations. Key valuation metrics, such as the price-to-earnings (P/E) ratio, price-to-book (P/B) ratio, and free cash flow yield, help investors determine whether a stock is overpriced, valued, or undervalued. Investing in a company with strong fundamentals but an excessively high valuation can lead to poor returns, even if the business itself remains successful.

Patience is a defining characteristic of great investors. Many people enter the market expecting quick results, only to become discouraged when stocks decline or remain stagnant. However, historical data shows that market downturns are temporary, while long-term growth is permanent.

The S&P 500, for example, has endured recessions, financial crises, and geopolitical instability, yet it has grown over 10,000% since its inception. Investors who stayed invested through past market crashes and corrections were rewarded with higher returns.

A critical aspect of long-term investing is staying disciplined during market volatility. It is natural for markets to fluctuate due to economic cycles, inflation fears, interest rate changes, or global uncertainties. However, making investment decisions based on short-term noise often leads to selling at the wrong time and missing recovery rallies. The ability to remain calm and committed to an investment thesis, even when markets are down, ensures that investors do not lock in unnecessary losses.

Regular portfolio reviews and rebalancing are necessary to maintain alignment with long-term goals. While the core strategy should remain intact, adjusting asset allocations based on life changes, risk tolerance, or economic shifts helps optimize performance. Investors should periodically reassess whether their investments continue to meet their original criteria. Selling underperforming assets that no longer have robust growth potential and reallocating to better opportunities enhances long-term returns.

Another key principle of long-term investing is focusing on cash flow and dividends. Companies that pay consistent and growing dividends tend to be financially stable and profitable, providing investors with both capital appreciation and passive income. Reinvesting dividends further accelerates compounding, increasing total portfolio value over time. Many of the most successful investors have built substantial wealth through dividend reinvestment strategies.

Investors must also develop mental resilience and emotional discipline. Stock market declines can trigger fear, leading many investors to sell at the worst possible time. Conversely, bull markets can create euphoria, causing investors to take excessive risks. Remaining unemotional and data-driven prevents costly mistakes. One of the most effective ways to build resilience is to view investing as owning businesses rather than trading stocks.

When investors adopt a business-owner mindset, they become less concerned with daily price fluctuations and more focused on the company's long-term growth potential.

Diversification remains essential for long-term success. While concentrating investments in a few high-growth stocks can lead to substantial gains, it also increases risk. A well-diversified portfolio containing growth stocks, dividend stocks, bonds, real estate, and international equities ensures stability across various market conditions. Exposure to different asset classes provides downside protection while still allowing capital to grow over time.

Investors should also recognize the importance of continuous learning and adaptation. Financial markets evolve, and industries change due to technological advancements, regulation, and consumer preferences. Staying informed about economic trends, industry shifts, and emerging investment opportunities helps investors make informed, future-proof decisions. Reading books, following expert analysis, and understanding macroeconomic trends contribute to better decision-making and portfolio management.

A long-term investing strategy does not mean ignoring market conditions or holding onto underperforming stocks indefinitely. While patience is vital, investors must also adapt and reassess when necessary. If a company's fundamentals deteriorate, its competitive position weakens, or added information suggests that its growth prospects have changed, adjusting the portfolio accordingly is a responsible action. Successful long-term investing requires both patience and the ability to recognize when change is needed.

Long-term wealth creation is built on discipline, consistency, and strategic decision-making. By following the principles of compounding, quality investing, emotional resilience, and adaptability, investors can navigate market cycles with confidence and achieve financial success. The greatest rewards come to those who can stay invested, make rational decisions, and allow time to work in their favour.

The journey to building lasting wealth is not about making quick trades or chasing trends—it is about owning great companies, managing risk effectively, and remaining committed to a long-term vision. Investors who embrace this philosophy will not only achieve financial freedom but will also create generational wealth that continues to grow for decades to come.

10.1 How to Stay Invested for the Long Run Without Letting Emotions Derail Your Strategy

Long-term investing requires more than just selecting the right stocks or building a diversified portfolio—it demands emotional resilience and a disciplined mindset. The greatest challenge most investors face is not market volatility, but their own emotions. Fear, greed, impatience, and overconfidence often lead to irrational decisions that can damage long-term financial success. Understanding how to manage emotions, stick to an investment strategy, and stay invested despite market fluctuations is what separates successful investors from those who underperform.

One of the most common mistakes investors make is reacting emotionally to market volatility. When markets are booming, greed takes over, leading many to chase overvalued stocks, convinced that prices will continue rising indefinitely. Conversely, during market downturns, fear dominates, causing investors to sell their holdings at a loss, thinking the market will never recover. History has proven that markets move in cycles, and those who panic during corrections often miss the best recovery opportunities.

Why Emotional Investing Leads to Poor Decisions

The financial markets are driven by investor psychology. Emotions such as fear and greed can cloud judgment and cause irrational actions, including:

- **Panic selling during downturns** – Investors see their portfolios declining and, fearing further losses, sell their investments at the worst possible time.
- **Chasing hot stocks** – When a stock is trending and prices are rising quickly, investors buy in due to FOMO (fear of missing out), often purchasing at inflated prices.
- **Holding onto losing investments too long** – Investors refuse to sell a stock that has dropped in value because they do not want to "admit defeat," even if the company's fundamentals have weakened.
- **Overtrading** – Making frequent changes to a portfolio based on short-term market movements rather than a well-thought-out investment plan.

Understanding these emotional tendencies is the first step in overcoming them. The key to staying invested for the long run is developing strategies to manage emotions and make decisions based on rational analysis rather than temporary market sentiment.

How to Develop an Emotionally Disciplined Investment Mindset

1. Shift Your Perspective from Stock Prices to Business Ownership

Many investors treat stocks like lottery tickets, focusing only on price fluctuations. However, the most successful long-term investors see themselves as part-owners of real businesses. Instead of checking daily stock prices, focus on the fundamentals of the companies you invest in. Ask yourself:

- Is the business growing its revenue and earnings over time?
- Does the company have a strong competitive advantage in its industry?
- Is the company well-managed with a solid balance sheet?

If the answer is yes, short-term price movements are irrelevant. Stocks fluctuate daily, but strong businesses generate real value over years and decades.

2. Create a Written Investment Plan and Stick to It

A structured investment plan removes emotions from decision-making. Your plan should outline:

- Your financial goals (e.g., retirement, wealth accumulation, passive income)
- Target asset allocation (stocks, bonds, real estate, cash)
- Criteria for buying and selling stocks.
- Rebalancing strategy and review intervals

Having a clear roadmap ensures that you are making investment decisions based on logic rather than fear or excitement. Whenever market volatility occurs, refer to your plan rather than reacting impulsively.

3. Ignore Short-Term Market Noise and Media Hype

Financial news is designed to create fear and excitement because dramatic headlines attract viewers. Constantly watching financial news or checking stock prices multiple times a day can led to unnecessary anxiety and impulsive actions.

To stay focused on long-term growth:
- Limit portfolio checkins to once a month or once a quarter rather than daily.
- Avoid making decisions based on media headlines or temporary market sentiment.
- Follow economic fundamentals and long-term trends rather than reacting to short-term volatility.

4. Automate Your Investments to Remove Emotion

One of the most effective ways to stay invested regardless of market conditions is to automate your investment contributions. Strategies like dollar-cost averaging (DCA) ensure that you are consistently buying into the market over time, reducing the impact of short-term fluctuations.

For example, if you invest $500 every month into an index fund, you will automatically buy more shares when prices are low and fewer shares when prices are high, leading to a better overall average purchase price.

Automation prevents emotional decision-making by removing the temptation to time the market.

5. Prepare Mentally for Market Corrections and Bear Markets

Market downturns are inevitable. Historically, the stock market has had 10% correction every 1-2 years and a bear market (20% or more drop) every 5-7 years. Yet, the market has always recovered and reached new highs.

- Instead of fearing downturns, expect them as part of the investment journey. Develop the mindset that:
- Corrections are buying opportunities to acquire quality stocks at lower prices.
- Bear markets are temporary, and long-term investors benefit from staying invested.
- Market timing is impossible, so the best strategy is to remain consistent.
- If you are mentally prepared for volatility, you will not panic when it happens.

6. Rebalance Periodically But Avoid Overtrading

While long-term investing does not mean ignoring your portfolio, constant buying and selling based on short-term movements reduces overall returns. Instead of reacting emotionally to price swings, follow a structured approach:

- Rebalance your portfolio every 6 to 12 months to maintain asset allocation.
- Sell only when an investment no longer meets your criteria, not because of temporary price declines.
- Add to positions in fundamentally strong companies when market corrections offer discounts.

7. Keep a Long-Term Perspective

The most successful investors are those who hold investments for decades, allowing compounding to generate exponential growth. If you invest $10,000 today and earn an 8% annual return, your portfolio will grow to $100,000 in 30 years. However, if you panic during downturns and sell early, you lose the power of long-term compounding.

Adopt the mindset of legendary investors like Warren Buffett, who famously said, "The stock market is designed to transfer money from the impatient to the patient." Those who remain committed to their strategy through bull and bear markets will see the best results.

The Key to Long-Term Investing Success

Mastering long-term investing is not just about choosing the right stocks—it is about controlling emotions, following a disciplined strategy, and staying committed despite market fluctuations. The investors who achieve financial success are not the ones who try to outguess the market but those who remain consistent, patient, and focused on the bigger picture. By developing an emotionally disciplined approach, automating investments, maintaining a long-term mindset, and ignoring short-term noise, you can build lasting wealth and financial security without being swayed by fear or greed. The ability to stay invested for the long run is what separates those who succeed from those who struggle in the stock market.

10.2 How to Identify and Hold High-Quality Investments for Decades

Long-term investing is not just about staying in the market—it is about owning the right businesses that can grow and generate wealth over decades. While market trends, fads, and speculative opportunities may offer short-term excitement, the most successful investors focus on finding fundamentally strong companies and holding onto them for the long haul. Identifying high-quality investments requires a deep understanding of financial health, competitive advantages, industry positioning, and long-term growth potential.

The best long-term investments are those that can compound wealth over time, withstand economic downturns, and remain relevant in changing market conditions. Investors who successfully hold these types of businesses benefit from consistent growth, reinvested earnings, and the power of compounding returns.

What Makes an Investment High-Quality?

A high-quality company is one that can generate increasing revenues, sustain profitability, and expand market share over time. These businesses often share the following characteristics:

- **Strong Competitive Advantage (Economic Moat)** – The company has barriers that protect it from competition, such as brand strength, patents, cost advantages, or network effects.
- **Consistent Revenue and Earnings Growth** – The company demonstrates steady top-line and bottom-line expansion over multiple years.
- **Strong Balance Sheet and Low Debt** – Companies with manageable debt and high liquidity are more resilient during economic downturns.
- **High Return on Invested Capital (ROIC)** – Efficient capital allocation leads to sustained profitability and reinvestment in future growth.

- **Industry Leadership and Market Dominance** – Companies that are leaders in their sector tend to outperform competitors and maintain pricing power.
- **Long-Term Vision and Innovation** – Businesses that invest in research, technology, and adaptation remain relevant in evolving markets.

Step 1: Evaluating a Company's Competitive Advantage

One of the most crucial factors in determining a company's long-term potential is its economic moat. A company with a strong competitive advantage can fend off competitors, maintain pricing power, and continue expanding without constant threats to its market position.

Examples of competitive advantages include:

- **Brand Strength** – Companies like Apple, Nike, and Coca-Cola have global recognition that allows them to charge premium prices.
- **Network Effects** – Businesses like Visa, Mastercard, and Google become stronger as more users join their platforms.
- **Cost Leadership** – Companies like Amazon and Walmart dominate through economies of scale, offering lower prices than competitors.
- **Switching Costs** – Enterprises like Microsoft and Adobe create products that businesses and consumers rely on, making it difficult to switch to competitors.
-

Step 2: Analysing Financial Health and Profitability

A company's financial strength determines whether it can survive economic downturns, invest in future growth, and reward shareholders over time. Several key metrics helps evaluate a company's financial health:

- **Revenue Growth** – A steady increase in sales over multiple years indicates a company's ability to expand its business.
- **Earnings Growth** – Rising net income suggests a company is effectively managing costs and improving profitability.
- **Profit Margins** – High and stable margins indicate strong pricing power and cost efficiency.
- **Return on Equity (ROE) and Return on Invested Capital (ROIC)** – These ratios show how efficiently a company uses capital to generate profits.

- **Debt-to-Equity Ratio** – A lower ratio means the company relies less on borrowed money, reducing financial risk.

Companies with strong financials tend to outlast economic downturns, invest in future expansion, and provide stable long-term returns.

Step 3: Investing in Companies with Sustainable Growth Potential

Identifying companies with long-term growth potential ensures that investments continue compounding for decades. High-quality businesses typically:

- Operate in expanding industries with strong demand.
- Reinvest profits into new products, technology, or acquisitions.
- Have a global presence or ability to scale operations beyond their current markets.
- Continuously adapt to market trends and changing consumer needs.

For example, technology, healthcare, renewable energy, and e-commerce are industries expected to grow significantly in the coming decades. Companies within these sectors that demonstrate consistent innovation, adaptability, and strong financials make ideal long-term investments.

Step 4: Avoiding Common Pitfalls When Choosing Long-Term Investments

Many investors fall into traps when selecting stocks for long-term holdings. Some common mistakes include:

- **Chasing Hype and Speculation** – Buying stocks based on temporary trends without evaluating fundamentals often leads to losses.
- **Ignoring Valuation** – Overpaying for even the best company can result in underperformance if the stock is significantly overvalued.
- **Neglecting Industry Disruptions** – Companies that fail to innovate or keep up with competitors may lose their advantage over time.
- **Focusing Only on Past Performance** – A stock's historical growth does not guarantee future success; investors should analyse future potential.

By avoiding these mistakes and focusing on businesses with strong fundamentals and durable competitive advantages, investors improve their chances of holding quality investments for decades.

Step 5: Holding Investments Through Market Cycles

The key to long-term investing is patience and conviction. Even the strongest companies will experience stock price volatility, but successful investors stay focused on the company's fundamentals rather than short-term price movements.

- **Market Crashes Create Buying Opportunities** – Instead of panic-selling, investors should use downturns to accumulate shares of high-quality businesses at lower prices.
- **Avoid Checking Prices Daily** – Constant monitoring can lead to emotional reactions and unnecessary trading.
- **Think Like a Business Owner** – Viewing investments as ownership in real businesses helps investors remain focused on long-term growth.

Investors who held companies like Amazon, Apple, and Microsoft through economic crises, stock price drops, and industry disruptions have seen significant returns over decades. The secret was understanding the company's strength and not selling out of fear.

The Power of Holding High-Quality Investments

Successful long-term investing is not about picking stocks at the perfect time—it is about identifying exceptional businesses and holding onto them through market cycles. The best investments generate wealth over decades by continuously growing revenue, profits, and market influence.

By focusing on fundamentally strong companies with competitive advantages, financial stability, and sustainable growth potential, investors can build a portfolio that withstands economic fluctuations and delivers superior returns over time.

Patience, discipline, and conviction in well-researched investments are the keys to compounding wealth and achieving long-term financial success.

10.3 How to Make Strategic Adjustments Without Disrupting Long-Term Growth

Long-term investing does not mean ignoring your portfolio indefinitely. While the foundation of a successful investment strategy is holding quality assets for decades, investors must still make strategic adjustments to adapt to market changes, economic cycles, and personal financial goals. The key is to optimize investments without overreacting to short-term volatility, ensuring that adjustments enhance long-term growth rather than disrupt it.

Many investors struggle with finding the balance between patience and adaptability. On one hand, making too many changes based on short-term price fluctuations can lead to poor decision-making and unnecessary trading costs. On the other hand, failing to adjust, when necessary, can result in holding underperforming assets or missing better opportunities. The best approach is to develop a structured process for reviewing and adjusting a portfolio while maintaining a long-term mindset.

When to Adjust Your Portfolio (and When to Stay the Course)

Understanding when to make changes and when to remain patient is one of the most important skills in investing. Some situations call for adjustments, while others require discipline to ride out temporary market fluctuations.

Scenarios That Require Strategic Adjustments

- **Significant Changes in a Company's Fundamentals** – If an investment's core business deteriorates, with declining earnings, loss of competitive advantage, or poor management decisions, it may be time to sell and reinvest elsewhere.
- **Major Life Events or Financial Changes** – If an investor's financial goals change due to marriage, retirement, or career shifts, adjusting asset allocation may be necessary.
- **Market Conditions That Affect Asset Allocation** – If a certain sector becomes overvalued or a market correction creates opportunities, investors may rebalance to take advantage of better risk-reward ratios.
- **Consistent Underperformance Compared to Peers** – If a stock or fund consistently lags its industry without a clear path to recovery, it might be time to replace it with a stronger alternative.

Scenarios Where Investors Should Stay the Course

- **Market Corrections or Temporary Declines** – Stock prices fluctuate, but short-term drops do not mean a company's long-term prospects have changed.
- **News Hype and Market Noise** – Headlines about inflation, interest rates, or political uncertainty often cause short-term market swings that do not

require portfolio changes.

- **Fear-Based Reactions During Bear Markets** – Selling during a downturn lock in losses. Unless a company's fundamentals have deteriorated, it is usually better to hold or even buy more at discounted prices.

By distinguishing between temporary market movements and real reasons for adjustment, investors avoid making changes based on emotions rather than strategy.

How to Adjust Your Portfolio Without Disrupting Growth

Once an investor identifies a valid reason for adjusting, it is important to do so in a way that minimizes risk, tax consequences, and unnecessary trading costs. The following methods ensure that changes are made strategically and efficiently.

1. Rebalancing to Maintain a Strong Asset Allocation

Over time, certain investments will outperform others, causing the portfolio to drift away from its original asset allocation. For example, if stocks have surged in value while bonds have remained stable, a portfolio that was initially 70% stocks and 30% bonds might shift to 85% stocks and 15% bonds, increasing risk exposure.

Rebalancing ensures that an investor maintains their preferred risk level. The process involves:

- Selling a portion of overperforming assets and reallocating to underweighted areas.
- Adding new capital to underweight asset classes instead of selling to minimize tax consequences.
- Rebalancing on a set schedule (quarterly, semi-annually, or annually) rather than reacting to market swings.

By regularly rebalancing, investors lock in gains from outperforming sectors and reinvest in undervalued areas, keeping the portfolio diversified and aligned with financial goals.

2. Gradually Adjusting Positions Instead of Making Drastic Changes

When adjusting, investors should avoid sudden, extreme moves that could disrupt long-term compounding. Instead of selling substantial portions of a portfolio at once, making small, incremental changes reduces risk and allows for better decision-making.

- If an investor wants to exit an underperforming stock, they can sell gradually over time rather than all at once.
- If shifting into a new sector, buying in phases rather than making a large purchase ensures better average entry prices.
- If reducing stock exposure before retirement, adjusting allocations over several years helps avoid market timing risks.

Taking a measured approach to portfolio adjustments ensures that investors do not overreact to temporary trends or sacrifice long-term gains.

3. Using Tax-Efficient Strategies When Selling or Reallocating

Whenever an investor sells assets, capital gains taxes can impact returns, especially in taxable accounts. To adjust while reducing tax liabilities:

- Prioritize tax-advantaged accounts (IRAs, 401(k)s) for rebalancing, where gains are not immediately taxed.
- Use tax-loss harvesting by selling underperforming assets at a loss to offset taxable gains.
- Hold investments for over a year to qualify for lower long-term capital gains tax rates.

Strategic tax planning ensures that portfolio adjustments do not erode investment returns due to unnecessary taxation.

4. Monitoring Industry Trends and Emerging Opportunities

While long-term investors should avoid chasing short-term fads, staying informed about industry trends allows for intelligent portfolio adjustments. Some industries naturally evolve over time, and companies that once dominated may lose their edge.

For example:

- The rise of e-commerce disrupted traditional retail, making companies like Amazon stronger while weakening brick-and-mortar stores.
- The shift toward renewable energy is challenging fossil fuel companies, increasing long-term potential for solar and electric vehicle industries.
- Advances in artificial intelligence and automation are transforming technology sectors, creating new investment opportunities.

Investors should evaluate whether their holdings still align with future growth trends. If a company or sector is losing its competitive advantage, reallocating capital into stronger industries can enhance long-term returns.

5. Maintaining a Core-Satellite Approach

One effective way to adjust without disrupting a long-term portfolio is using a core-satellite strategy. This approach involves:

Keeping a core portfolio of stable, long-term investments (index funds, blue-chip stocks, dividend payers).

Using a smaller portion of the portfolio for tactical adjustments to explore emerging opportunities or short-term trends.

For example, an investor may allocate 80% of their portfolio to a diversified mix of stocks and bonds while using the remaining 20% for high-growth stocks, sector rotations, or alternative assets. This allows for flexibility without compromising overall portfolio stability.

Adjusting While Staying Committed to Growth

Long-term investing requires both patience and adaptability. While investors should resist the temptation to overtrade or react emotionally to market fluctuations, ignoring necessary adjustments can also hinder portfolio growth. The key is to make strategic, well-reasoned changes that enhance stability and optimize performance over time. By regularly reviewing asset allocation, using tax-efficient strategies, monitoring industry shifts, and maintaining a core-satellite balance, investors can adapt to changing market conditions without sacrificing long-term wealth accumulation. The most successful investors stay committed to their strategy while remaining flexible enough to seize opportunities and mitigate risks. Adjusting with discipline and foresight ensures that a portfolio continues growing for decades, securing financial stability and long-term success.

Conclusion:

The Path to Long-Term Wealth and Financial Freedom

Investing is not just about choosing the right stocks or making quick gains—it is about building a disciplined, long-term strategy that withstands market cycles, economic shifts, and personal financial changes. Throughout this book, we have explored the essential principles of selecting quality investments, managing risk, and staying committed to long-term growth. Now, as we reach the conclusion, it is important to reflect on the key lessons that will guide you toward financial security and wealth accumulation for years to come. The most successful investors share one common trait: patience. The ability to remain invested, avoid emotional decision-making, and allow compounding to work over decades is what separates those who build wealth from those who struggle with inconsistent returns. Market fluctuations, economic downturns, and financial news cycles will always create distractions, but sticking to a well-defined investment strategy ensures that these short-term events do not derail long-term success.

A well-constructed portfolio is one that is diversified, resilient, and aligned with your financial goals. Throughout this book, we have discussed the importance of:

- Investing in fundamentally strong companies with durable competitive advantages.
- Maintaining a diversified portfolio that balances growth and stability.
- Avoiding emotional decision-making by following a structured investment plan.
- Using tax-efficient strategies to maximize after-tax returns.
- Making strategic adjustments, when necessary, but avoiding unnecessary overtrading.

By implementing these strategies, you create a financial foundation that can weather any market condition while continuously growing your wealth.

Embracing the Long-Term Investor Mindset

One of the biggest challenges investors faces is staying committed during volatile times. It is easy to feel confident when markets are rising, but when downturns occur, many investors panic and abandon their strategy. However, history has shown that those who remain patient and invested through market corrections benefit the most. Consider the S&P 500: Despite recessions, financial crises, and economic uncertainty, it has consistently reached new all-time highs over the long term. Investors who stayed the course and continued investing during downturns saw significant long-term gains, while those who panicked and sold locked in losses. Long-term investing is not about predicting short-term movements but about owning quality assets that grow over time. Your goal as an investor is not to react to every market swing, but to build a portfolio that compounds wealth steadily over decades.

The Role of Discipline and Continuous Learning

Investing is a lifelong journey. Markets evolve, industries shift, and economic conditions change. The best investors are those who continuously educate themselves, adapt to new opportunities, and remain disciplined in their approach. Staying informed about emerging trends, technological advancements, and economic policies will help refine your strategy and ensure that your investments remain well-positioned for future growth. At the same time, discipline is key. The temptation to chase speculative stocks, time the market, or deviate from your long-term plan will always be present. But by maintaining a rational, structured approach to investing, you eliminate emotional decision-making and maximize your chances of long-term success.

Your Financial Future is in Your Hands

The principles outlined in this book are not just strategies for investing—they are a blueprint for financial independence. By applying these lessons, you can create a portfolio that:

- Grows steadily over time through compounding.
- Provides financial security for you and your family.
- Generates passive income through dividends and reinvestments.
- Ensures resilience during market downturns and economic uncertainty.

Your financial future is not determined by luck or market timing—it is shaped by the actions you take today. Whether you are just starting your investment journey or refining an existing strategy, the key to success is staying committed, remaining patient, and making smart, informed decisions. The road to long-term wealth requires discipline, perseverance, and a willingness to stick with your strategy even when the market evaluates your resolve. Those who embrace these principles will not only achieve financial freedom but will also build a legacy of wealth that lasts for generations.

Now, the next step is yours. Start investing, stay invested, and let time work in your favour.

www.ingramcontent.com/pod-product-compliance
Lightning Source LLC
Chambersburg PA
CBHW081506200326
41518CB00015B/2395